Palgrave Macmillan Studies in Family and Intimate Life

Series Editors
Graham Allan
Keele University
Keele, United Kingdom

Lynn Jamieson
University of Edinburgh
Edinburgh, United Kingdom

David H.J. Morgan
University of Manchester
Manchester, United Kingdom

'The Palgrave Macmillan Studies in Family and Intimate Life series is impressive and contemporary in its themes and approaches' - Professor Deborah Chambers, Newcastle University, UK, and author of *New Social Ties*.

The remit of the Palgrave Macmillan Studies in Family and Intimate Life series is to publish major texts, monographs and edited collections focusing broadly on the sociological exploration of intimate relationships and family organization. The series covers a wide range of topics such as partnership, marriage, parenting, domestic arrangements, kinship, demographic change, intergenerational ties, life course transitions, step-families, gay and lesbian relationships, lone-parent households, and also non-familial intimate relationships such as friendships and includes works by leading figures in the field, in the UK and internationally, and aims to contribute to continue publishing influential and prize-winning research.

More information about this series at
http://www.springer.com/series/14676

Anna Sparrman • Allan Westerling • Judith Lind • Karen Ida Dannesboe
Editors

Doing Good Parenthood

Ideals and Practices of Parental Involvement

Editors
Anna Sparrman
Department of Thematic Studies – Child
Studies
Linköping University
Linköping, Sweden

Allan Westerling
Center for Childhood, Youth &
Family Research, Department of People &
Technology
Roskilde University
Roskilde, Denmark

Judith Lind
Department of Thematic Studies – Child
Studies
Linköping University
Linköping, Sweden

Karen Ida Dannesboe
Department of Educational Anthropology
School of Education
Aarhus University
Aarhus, Denmark

Palgrave Macmillan Studies in Family and Intimate Life
ISBN 978-3-319-46773-3   ISBN 978-3-319-46774-0 (eBook)
DOI 10.1007/978-3-319-46774-0

Library of Congress Control Number: 2016960731

Cover illustration: Pattern adapted from an Indian cotton print produced in the 19th century

Printed on acid-free paper

This Palgrave Macmillan imprint is published by Springer Nature
The registered company is Springer International Publishing AG
The registered company address is: Gewerbestrasse 11, 6330 Cham, Switzerland

ACKNOWLEDGEMENTS

The idea for this book on parenthood was first born in 2013 during a meeting of the Nordic Network of Child Researchers held at Linköping University, Sweden. Researchers from Sweden, Denmark and Norway met to discuss the current state and future direction of Nordic academic research about children and childhood. From this larger body of researchers, a smaller group from Denmark and Sweden interested in family, parenthood and the welfare state crystallised.

The members of the group soon discovered that, despite our different research topics, we shared an interest in the normative aspects of parenthood. Right there, in Linköping, we decided to plan a joint publication to bring together knowledge about good parenthood. Simultaneously, we decided to hold a session at the Conference of the European Society of Family Relations in Madrid in 2014. The session was a great success, and we would like to thank Esther Dermott for helpful feedback on our papers and the rest of the session participants for contributing to a good and constructive discussion. As we identified shared themes, theoretical interests, empirical sites and analytical perspectives, an intricate complexity of parenthood took shape. The common denominator behind these shared elements seemed to be heterogeneous norms of parenthood in specific settings and situations. Slowly, we developed the concept of *doing good parenthood* that is the focus of this book. Texts, abstracts, titles and ideas were circulated between authors and editors with the aim of making *doing good parenthood* central to the analyses. As a result, the book presents a very broad and complex set of practices of parenthood. The normativity of parenthood presented in the ten chapters highlight at least ten versions of what good parenthood can mean.

We would like to thank all the people – children, parents, teachers, social workers – who have been involved in the different research projects. Without you, our ideas and thoughts would not have been challenged and this contribution to knowledge about parenthood would not have been developed. We would also like to extend our warmest thanks to all the contributing authors for their patience, hard work and faith in this project. The editors have met and worked together on several occasions. We looked for a venue located an equal distance from Roskilde, Copenhagen and Linköping in order to save travel time. Professor Lars Plantin of Malmö University kindly offered his help, by allowing us to meet face to face in his department of Social Work. This has been invaluable in assisting us to finish the book! The friendship and support of our Nordic colleagues have been important for the completion of this book, as has Liz Sourbut's, Nancy Aaen's and Nicholas Wrigley's linguistic editing.

Our most sincere gratitude goes to Professor Esther Dermott. Firstly, for being the commentator on our papers at the Madrid conference in 2014. Secondly, and more importantly, we want to express our appreciation for you for having taken on the great task of commenting on the book in the last chapter. In this way, the analysis extends beyond the Swedish and Danish agenda and situates the doing of good parenthood within a wider international context. Thank you!

We are very pleased that Palgrave Macmillan decided to publish this book in their Studies in Families and Intimate Life series as we think that it has the potential to inspire further thinking about both good parenthood and good childhood, and how these concepts relate to one another.

The publication of this book has been made possible by individual research grants and great support from the academic departments of the four editors.

Contents

Contributors

Maria Ørskov Akselvoll Center for Childhood, Youth & Family Research, Department of People & Technology, Roskilde University, Roskilde, Denmark

Dil Bach Department of Educational Anthropology, School of Education, Aarhus University, Aarhus, Denmark

Disa Bergnehr School of Health and Welfare, Jönköping University, Jönköping, Sweden

David Cardell Department of Sociology, Örebro University, Örebro, Sweden

Karen Ida Dannesboe Department of Educational Anthropology, School of Education, Aarhus University, Aarhus, Denmark

Esther Dermott School of Sociology, Politics and International Studies, University of Bristol, Bristol, UK

Pernille Juhl Center for Childhood, Youth & Family Research, Department of People & Technology, Roskilde University, Roskilde, Denmark

Judith Lind Department of Thematic Studies – Child Studies, Linköping University, Linköping, Sweden

Anne-Li Lindgren Department of Child and Youth Studies, Stockholm University, Stockholm, Sweden

Cecilia Lindgren Department of Thematic Studies – Child Studies, Linköping University, Linköping, Sweden

Anna Malmquist Department of Behavioural Sciences and Learning, Linköping University, Linköping, Sweden

Anna Polski Department of Psychology, Lund University, Lund, Sweden

Tobias Samuelsson School of Education and Communication, Jönköping University, Jönköping, Sweden

Anna Sparrman Department of Thematic Studies – Child Studies, Linköping University, Linköping, Sweden

Allan Westerling Center for Childhood, Youth & Family Life Research, Department of People & Technology, Roskilde, Denmark

Karin Zetterqvist Nelson Department of Thematic Studies – Child Studies, Linköping University, Linköping, Sweden

LIST OF FIGURES

CHAPTER 1

Introduction: Doing Good Parenthood

Judith Lind, Allan Westerling, Anna Sparrman
and Karen Ida Dannesboe

Abstract The purpose of this book is to explore in ten empirical chapters how good parenthood is done in different contexts, by different agents. The introductory chapter outlines the theoretical implications of viewing parenthood as a series of practices and our interest in the enactment and negotiation of good parenthood. We argue that the doing of good parenthood should be studied empirically and in context. Therefore, the particularities of Denmark and Sweden as contexts are briefly introduced. Finally, we argue that parenthood is to be understood in relation to childhood, and the doing of good parenthood

J. Lind (✉) · A. Sparrman
Department of Thematic Studies – Child Studies, Linköping University,
Linköping, Sweden
e-mail: judith.lind@liu.se; anna.sparrman@liu.se

A. Westerling
Center for Childhood, Youth & Family Life Research, Department
of People & Technology, Roskilde University, Roskilde, Denmark
e-mail: allanw@ruc.dk

K.I. Dannesboe
Department of Educational Anthropology, School of Education, Aarhus
University, Aarhus, Denmark
e-mail: kida@edu.au.dk

1

should be situated in relation to notions of children's interests and rights. Therefore, the book is anchored in the research fields of both parenting studies and child studies.

Keywords Good parenthood · Childhood · Qualitative methods · Parenthood · Childhood studies · Doing parenthood · Parenthood-childhood

This book is an exploration of parenthood. The overall aim is to study both the ideals and practices of parenthood without separating the two aspects. We do so in ten empirical chapters by analysing how good parenthood is done in ten different contexts, by different agents. Across these chapters, we will investigate the normative layers of parenthood in practice.

We have deliberately chosen to use the term *parenthood*, rather than *parenting*, as our focus is not only on practices; it is broader. Our theoretical point of departure is informed by David Morgan's concept of family practices and his ambition to move "away from ideas of the family as relative static structures or sets of positions or statuses" (Morgan 2011, 6; See also Cheal 2002). Parenthood, in a similar manner, is something that is done. We see it as a series of practices, as something that men, women and children do. This comprises much more than merely the child-rearing practices of parents. Parenthood, we argue, is also done when parents interact with others; for example, professionals like teachers or social workers, with other parents, including co-parents, or grandparents. When parents argue in favour of their strategies, when they negotiate with an ex-partner, when they conform to (or refuse) the demands placed upon them by schools, when they consume goods or choose destinations for family outings, parenthood is being done.

One component of parenthood is the parent's desire to do a good job according to her/his own standards. In the doing of parenthood in front of an audience (Finch 2007) another component is at play: parents' desire to be recognised as good parents by others (Blackford 2004; Caputo 2007). In the doing of parenthood in a specific situation, norms are mobilised through parents' own views of what good parenthood is, what they believe are the parenthood norms of the audience and the audience's reactions to certain practices. The audience or co-actors such as other parents, children, professionals, politicians, experts and researchers for that matter, also do parenthood. This is an important part of the reasoning behind our choice to use this term rather than parenting.

What are the standards by which parenthood is evaluated? As the analysis will show, good parenthood is not fixed or stable; in practice, it is rather fluid and subject to negotiation. Not only is the meaning of the best interests of the child – often used as a benchmark for the evaluation of parenthood – ambiguous, but the best interests of the child are also not necessarily the only benchmark in play. The normative layers of parenthood are related to ideas about what constitutes a good childhood, family ideals, ideas about children's development and needs, as well as goals regarding a nation's public health, education and competitiveness.

When we explore how parenthood is done, we are also exploring how *good* parenthood is done. We study the contextual and situated practices through which the different actors – parents, children and others – do parenthood, and we also study the normative guidelines through which these practices become meaningful. Doing good parenthood refers to contextual and situated practices through which parents, children and others enact, negotiate and construct *the good* in good parenthood. Our interests thus include not only the meanings of good parenthood that float to the surface in these practices but also how the positioning of some parenting practices as good is achieved in and through such practices. Doing good parenthood, however, also refers to the doing of parenthood in relation to something that is predefined, or appears to be predefined, as good.

This book presents a broad set of empirically rich chapters to give the reader a detailed and deep understanding of what it means to *do good parenthood*. Across the chapters, we address the following questions: What does good parenthood come to mean in practice? By whom, where and through what practices is good parenthood defined? Who speaks on behalf of whom? What are the standards by which good parenthood is evaluated? Whose or what interests are emphasised? In all of these questions, the specific national and local contexts within which the practices that constitute the subjects of analyses are set are taken into consideration.

DENMARK AND SWEDEN AS POLITICAL CONTEXT

The primary context for our empirical studies are the Danish and Swedish welfare societies. The structures constituted by family policies contribute to shaping the conditions for negotiations of good parenthood, but they are to some extent also the products of such negotiations. Both Denmark and

Sweden represent a Scandinavian or universalistic welfare regime and a family policy that can be labelled pro-egalitarian, stressing gender equality and high rates of female employment (Esping-Andersen 1990, 1999). Both countries also have comparatively generous and flexible parental leave programmes, individual taxation of spouses and subsidised childcare (Béland et al. 2014). High levels of employment for both mothers and fathers and high rates of child enrolment in out-of-family childcare naturally limit the amount of time that Danish and Swedish parents spend with their children. Interestingly, parental involvement is still seen as crucial to children's development, and parents emphasise the value of spending quality time with their children, and preferably as a family, in both Denmark and Sweden. Using the term *involved parenthood*, Forsberg (2009) shows how Swedish parents strive to be involved in their children's lives by spending time on as well as with their children (see also Wissö 2012). Similar ideals of parental involvement can be found in Denmark (Dannesboe et al. 2012).

The emphasis on gender equality is part of social and family policies which emphasise individual autonomy. This supports the individualisation and democratisation of family life and comes close to the notion of institutionalised individualism (Beck and Beck-Gernsheim 2002), which is supported by family policy traditions characterised by an individualised relationship between the state and its citizens (including children) rather than by institutional support for the family as a unit or entity. These policies and the individualisation of family life are manifested most clearly through the strong legislative focus on children's rights. A prerequisite for this kind of individual autonomy has been a strong state, a high degree of trust in the institutions of the state and a relatively high level of acceptance of state intervention in the lives of families (Abrahamson 2010; Berggren and Trägårdh 2015; Wells and Bergnehr 2014).

However, in both countries, family policies have undergone notable changes during the last three decades. The early 1990s marked the beginning of an economic crisis that led to severe cut-backs in state-funded welfare provision, which coincided with a shift towards neoliberal rhetoric. The cuts were ideologically legitimised with the aid of such rhetoric, which emphasised freedom of choice, as opposed to the alleged demand for conformity of previous welfare service provision, and welcomed the introduction of private, market-based alternatives (Lundqvist 2011; Grumløse 2014). Yet, the focus on formal employment for both women and men in Sweden and Denmark has entailed a continued expansion of universal childcare, which continues to distinguish them from countries with liberal welfare models.

Even though the institutional fabric of the Danish and Swedish welfare states share many constitutive elements, there are also differences between the two countries' family policies. While an explicit gender-equal ideal of parenthood is shared across traditional political divisions in the Swedish Parliament (the current Swedish Prime Minister declaring himself a feminist), feminism is marginalised in mainstream Danish political discourses. This is most evident in the parental leave schemes. Although both countries strive to achieve gender equality, not only by increasing mothers' degree of employment in the formal labour market but also by increasing fathers' involvement in family life, Danish family policy can be described as a little less universal and less interventionist than Swedish policies (Abrahamson 2010; Lundqvist 2011).

PARENTING STUDIES

Parenting is, of course, a global phenomenon and parents rear children all over the world. Yet, it is also a historically and socially situated practice. This means that parents' aspirations for their children, as well as parenting ideals and practices, vary across different time periods, national contexts, cultures and local contexts. Thus, this book shares a common interest with the emerging field of parenting culture studies. Within this field, parenting is viewed as a cultural product and a historically and socially situated form of childrearing (Lee et al. 2014), and studies are concerned with the relationships between policy, experts and parents and the acknowledgement of certain predominant parenting styles and ideals (Faircloth et al. 2013).

However, this book also argues that parenthood cannot be understood without relating it to childhood, and therefore we also have a common interest with child studies, which will be discussed below.

Women's increased involvement in the labour market and the impact of paid work on family practices were central to the field of parenting studies during the 1970s and 1980s (Gatrell 2015; Gatrell et al. 2013). Therefore, the field initially focused on mothers and mothering. In 1996, American sociologist Sharon Hays (1996) described an ideology of *intensive mothering* that places the child at the centre of family life and expects the mother to be willing to expend a great deal of physical, emotional, cognitive and financial resources on the child and to put her children's needs above her own. As a result, intensive mothering as a dominant parenting ideal has been argued to affect societal attitudes towards working mothers as their paid work limits the amount of time that they are able to spend with their children (Gatrell et al. 2013). Since then, both mothers' and fathers' management of parenting (Smart and Neale 1999) and engaged involvement in their children's upbringing have received increased attention in parenting studies. Research on fathers and fatherhood shows that, across Europe, fathers engage in a wider range of childcare practices than previously reported, and recent research has introduced concepts like *intimate fathering* (Dermott 2008) and *reflexive fathering* (Westerling 2015). The aim behind the introduction of such concepts is to bring to the fore fathers' subjective orientation, along with their experiences and practices of parenting. Fathers have become more involved and engaged than earlier cultural stereotypes suggest (Dermott and Miller 2015).

The chapters of this book are set in the national and political contexts of Denmark and Sweden. These countries have a long tradition of women's participation in the labour market and high percentages of children's enrolment in childcare. Involved parenthood and time-intensive mothering, or fathering, must be understood in light of these traditions. Our claim is that any exploration of the doing of good parenthood must include the context in which that doing occurs.

While the importance of the role of the parent to ensure a successful outcome has a long history, the task of parenting has acquired particular connotations recently and is seen as requiring specific skills and levels of expertise (Faircloth et al. 2013; Lee et al. 2014). The idea that the development of children is more or less entirely determined by parents' choices and parenting practices, along with the referral to parenting as a key factor in explanations regarding social problems or educational failure, has been labelled *parental determinism* (Furedi 2002). While the idea of parents being a risk in children's lives is not new, the assumption of parental determinism has increased the perceived need in society to offer expert advice to parents and to assess parenting practices and their outcome for children's development. By adopting a language of developmental psychology, and thereby presenting itself as neutral and scientific, current discourse on parenting in many European countries gives the impression that what are regarded as preferable outcomes of parenting are universal and objective. This apparently scientific discourse presupposes a causal relationship between certain parenting behaviours and particular outcomes for children (Ramaekers and Suissa 2012). Critics speak of a politicisation of parenthood, in which parenting has been turned into the task of supplying the state with well-functioning citizens and in which parents are made responsible, not only for the health of their own children but also for the public health of the entire nation (cf. Lister 2008; Gillies 2012; Oelkers 2012; Shirani et al. 2012). Such a view on parenting precludes any ethical, moral or personal questions concerning what the goals of parenting should be. What is to be regarded as a preferable outcome of parenting is not, however, necessarily given (Arendt 2006). Any calculation of a child's best interests, and hence of what constitutes good parenthood, must be regarded as being screened through specific values. Questions about what makes human beings flourish, what kind of people we want our children to be or what kinds of relationships we want to promote are moral questions to which there are no fixed answers (Goodman 2008; Ramaekers and Suissa 2012). We argue that the varying answers given to these questions in different contexts must be studied empirically.

CHILD STUDIES AND PARENTHOOD

It is difficult to understand parenthood without relating it to childhood, simply because it is difficult to imagine a child without its relation to adults or to imagine parents without children (Jenks 1996). In our relation to the notion of parenthood, we bring with us the interdisciplinarity and multiplicity of child studies, which has inspired us to approach and explore parenthood as both a structural/discursive category, and/or with an interest in parents in practice (cf. Smith and Green 2014). We suggest that parenthood is a cultural phrasing of adulthood. In the same way as adults and children are defined through their mutual dependency (Prout 2005), childhood and parenthood cannot be understood independently of each other. In theoretical terms, the focus is on the plurality of parenthood – parenthood*s* – concentrating on the coexistence, changeability and situatedness of parenthood. By doing this, we argue that the multiple or even hybrid (Prout 2005) notion and approach to childhood(s) must be mirrored in how parenthood(s) is/ are recognised. We aim to show that the categories of children and parents, as well as childhood and parenthood, are not only intertwined but also shape one another.

One important aspect of the relationship between childhood and parenthood, and between children and parents, concerns dependence, including independence and interdependence. When the sociology of childhood emerged and was developed in the 1980s, it was as a critique against mainstream sociologists' lack of interest in children. Instead of viewing children primarily as members of families, they were seen as individuals in their own right equipped with agency, and as independent social actors (James and Prout 1990; James et al. 1998; Jenks 1996; Mayall 2013; Smith and Green 2014). Childhood sociologists were also critical of developmental psychology's notions of how children's behaviours and maturity follow a universal age-fixed developmental chart. Children, they argued, were to be acknowledged as competent beings, not merely as adults in becoming (James and Prout 1990).

The emphasis on children's agency paralleled the increased focus on children's rights, including the introduction of the UN Convention on the Rights of the Child (UNCRC 1989). Although the UNCRC does emphasise the role of parents by demanding that states respect their rights and duties (Article 5, UNCRC), stating children's right to be cared for by their parents (Article 7, UNCRC) and demanding that education is directed towards the development of respect for the child's parents (Article 29, UNCRC), the increased importance attributed to children's rights has had a constraining effect on the practices of parenthood. This has been particularly evident in Scandinavia, including Denmark and Sweden. Children's rights, some researchers argue, downplay children's dependency on their parents and simultaneously contribute to the responsibilisation of children (Smith 2012). Reviewing the construction of children as independent and mature agents within the sociology of childhood, some of its founders have recently argued for a more collectivist view of children, including their dependency on, and relation to, adults as well as for the necessity to acknowledge the significance of children's distinct biological and psychological features (Lee 1998; Prout 2005; See also Smith and Green 2014).

To some extent, children's rights also imply a potential conflict of interests between children and their parents, a conflict that warrants the kind of state intervention into family life on behalf of the child that characterises the Danish and Swedish family policy traditions. It presumes the ability of state authorities to specify the best interests of the child, perhaps better than parents, and to distinguish good from bad parenthood.

How to Read This Book

This book is a collection of empirical chapters that serve to explore and analyse how good parenthood is done. Through the analysis of empirical material, drawing on multiple approaches, methods and data, we develop our contribution to the discussion about the practices of contemporary parenthood. From a methodological point of view, *doing* good parenthood means focusing, with the help of qualitative methods, on practices within which parenthood is performed and defined. Qualitative methods make it possible to take into serious consideration the proposal that parenthood has no standard meaning but receives and creates norms and values in and through practices (cf. Van Blerk et al. 2009). There is no single qualitative research method that can help us to define or grasp what is meant by good parenthood. Instead, the chapters present a mixture of qualitative methods, including the analysis of political documents and computer-mediated communication as well as the collection of data through participant observation, interviewing, photography, and video recording. So how can we assert that what is going on in the practices that constitute the data for the chapters of this book is the doing of good parenthood? In the majority of chapters, either the situation as such or the participants themselves define that what is being done is good parenthood, for instance when parents give advice to other parents about parenting strategies. In other chapters, good parenthood is done in the interview situation, for example when teachers describe parental involvement. Doing good parenthood is explored through social practices and the narratives of parents, professionals and children and between researchers and participants in our empirical studies. The empirical data were originally collected for different and independent research projects during the period of 2000–2015 in which parenthood was either the explicit research topic or surfaced as an analytical category during research projects on family life or childhood.

All ten chapters pose the same questions: How is parenthood done? Through what practices is good parenthood constituted? Who defines what is good? In this sense, all the empirical chapters have a shared interest in how norms about parenthood are produced. The answers to these questions vary between the different chapters. The analyses show that different institutional practices place different demands and expectations on parents and in this sense the definition of good parenthood appears incoherent or ambivalent. Yet, this ambiguity is an important result of our analysis and the empirical chapters serve to illustrate and exemplify how different versions of parenthood coexist in the same, or similar, situations. The various chapters also demonstrate that very different actions may be demanded in different situations for parents to do good parenthood. The aim of the book is to preserve, stay with and elaborate upon the rich complexity of our empirical data. We have not searched for standardisations but have allowed ourselves to stay with the complex (cf. Law 2004).

While this clearly illustrates the ambiguity and complexity with which good parenthood is done in practice, it is also possible to identify certain aspects of parenthood that are recurrently construed as good. Together, the empirical chapters present the consequences of contemporary social change for families, parents and children in everyday life.

Across the chapters, a picture of good parenthood emerges. It does not appear as something static or uncontested but as a dynamic and ambiguous phenomenon constructed in discourse and practices in diverse social contexts in everyday life. Empirically, the chapters cover diverse social contexts such as families, online discussion boards, theme parks, and meetings between professionals, parents and children. Parents appear as a diverse group with different socio-economic and cultural backgrounds and in different family constructions such as nuclear families to single parents and same-sex parents. Most of the chapters focus on the parents themselves, and their practices and negotiations, discussions and narratives about being a parent (Ørskov Akselvoll, Bach, Juhl, Lind, Malmquist et al., Westerling). One chapter focuses on parents and children's shared leisure activities and their material context (Sparrman et al.), while another explores children's contributions to the constructions of good parenthood (Dannesboe). The role of professionals in doing good parenthood is also explored (Bergnehr, Lindgren).

Several of the chapters illustrate how professionals and experts play a central role in constructions of good parenthood. In particular, Cecilia Lindgren and Disa Bergnehr each analyse how good parenthood emerges from professionals' descriptions of parents in a Swedish context. Lindgren analyses social workers' assessment reports on prospective adoptive parents and illustrates how these reports establish certain understandings of what is required to be a good parent, while Bergnehr focuses on school professionals' discourses on good and poor parenting in disadvantaged areas. In other chapters, professionals' attitudes and practices serve as a backdrop to understanding how their instructions impact on parenting practices (Juhl) and differences between professionals' and children's perspectives on parental involvement in schools (Dannesboe). In different ways, these chapters illustrate how professionals contribute to a standardisation of what counts as good parenthood, for example be involved, to provide regularity, and to spend (enough) time with your child. But, as Bergnehr emphasises, the school professionals in her study are aware that there can be different reasons why parents do not act as good, involved parents in school.

A central theme across the chapters concerns time: how much time parents spend with their children and how parents and children share and use time. Making time for children and spending time with children seems to be a sacrifice that parents make, but also a right. For instance, Allan Westerling emphasises that separated parents assert that spending time with their children is also an entitlement, reflecting an ideal of reciprocity where time with the children is distributed equally between the divorced parents. Additionally, Lindgren and Westerling emphasise that good parenthood is about sacrifice, giving up what the parents want or what they want to spend time on as adults to focus on the needs of their children. Prioritising time with the children also seems to correspond with norms of being a child-centred parent, choosing activities with and for children. Parents and children spending time together is also a focal point in Anna Sparrman et al.'s chapter on togetherness during family visits to child cultural establishments such as children's museums, theme parks and amusement parks. Taking the physical surroundings and material objects (such as mobile phones and wallets) into consideration, the authors analyse how family togetherness is done through distance and proximity between children and parents while visiting child-oriented child-cultural establishments.

Another focus is on parenting strategies and forms of parental involvement in children's and teenagers' lives. Judith Lind's chapter illustrates how good parenthood is constructed and negotiated by Swedish parents in online discussion groups, in which parents give each other advice about parental strategies in relation to teenagers, alcohol and sex. This discussion illustrates diverse parenting strategies, from regulating behaviours and setting limits to letting go and respecting the privacy of teenagers. The discussions among parents also show how parenting strategies must be justified. The choices you make as a parent and the need to justify your decisions is also a common theme in Pernille Juhl's chapter, which explores parenting practices among marginalised families subject to interventions by child protection services. It is also highlighted in

Anna Malmquist et al. chapter on Swedish lesbian couples' use of permanently anonymous donors. This chapter demonstrates how constructions of the role of the donor as *the donor is not the father* or *the donor is the child's other half* serve as a way to position themselves as good parents.

Changing norms of parenthood in educational reforms, in institutions and among professionals and parents themselves illustrate how changes in what counts as good parenthood contribute to the development of diverse and even contrasting norms. The chapters address the ways in which schools, professionals and educational reforms promote certain ideals of proper parenthood and how these ideals correspond with or challenge parents' practices and understandings. Exploring the digital involvement of parents from diverse socio-economic backgrounds in their children's school, Maria Ørskov Akselvoll suggests that the school serves as a gatekeeper to good parenthood. Karen Ida Dannesboe's study of school children and relations between school and family discusses how children's ideals of good (school) parents differs from dominant norms of parental involvement produced by teachers. Dil Bach's study is concerned with educational reforms and parenting practices in Denmark and Singapore. Her study suggests that shared perceptions of global competition have led to mirroring processes, resulting in reverse educational reforms and changes in parenting norms.

To sum up, this book presents a broad set of empirically rich chapters, which gives the reader a detailed and deep understanding of what it means to do good parenthood. Through the multitude of contexts, practices and social actors presented in the various chapters, the complexity of good parenthood is illustrated. Serving primarily as empirical explorations of how good parenthood is done, the chapters rely for their theoretical grounding on this introduction and the synthesis presented in Professor Esther Dermott's concluding chapter. Hence, although the book is presented as an anthology, with chapters authored by different researchers, it should be considered, and if possible read, as a cohesive whole.

References

Abrahamson, P. 2010. "Continuity and consensus. Governing families in Denmark." *Journal of European Social Policy* 25(5): 399–409.

Arendt, H. 2006. *Between past and future*. New York: Penguin Group.

Beck, U., and E. Beck-Gernsheim. 2002. *Individualization*. London: Sage Publications.

Béland, D., P. Blomqvist, J.G. Andersen, J. Palme and A. Waddan. 2014. "The universal decline of universality? Social policy change in Canada, Denmark, Sweden and the UK." *Social Policy and Administration* 48(7): 739–756.

Berggren, H., and L. Trägårdh. 2015. *Är svensken människa? Gemenskap och oberoende i det moderna Sverige* [Are Swedes humans? Community and independence in modern Sweden]. Stockholm: Norstedts.

Blackford, H. 2004. "Playground Panopticism." *Childhood* 12(1): 431–447.

Caputo, V. 2007. "She's from a 'good family': Performing childhood and motherhood in a Canadian private school setting." *Childhood* 14(2): 173–192.

Cheal, D. 2002. *Sociology of family life.* Basingstoke: Palgrave Macmillan.

Dannesboe, K.I., N. Kryger, C. Palludan and B. Ravn. 2012. *Hvem sagde samarbejde? Et Hverdagslivsstudie af skole-hjem-relationer* [Who said cooperation? An everyday life study of school-home relations]. Aarhus: Aarhus Universitetsforlag.

Dermott, E. 2008. *Intimate fatherhood: A sociological analysis.* London, New York: Routledge, Taylor & Francis Group.

Dermott, E., and T. Miller. 2015. "More than the sum of its parts? Contemporary fatherhood policy, practice and discourse." *Families, Relationships and Societies* 4(2): 183–195.

Esping-Andersen, G. 1990. *The three worlds of welfare capitalism.* Cambridge: Polity Press.

Esping-Andersen, G. 1999. *Social foundations of post-industrial economies.* Oxford: Oxford University Press.

Faircloth, C., D. Hoffman, and L. Layne, eds. 2013. *Parenting in global perspective: Negotiating ideologies of kinship, self and politics.* New York: Routledge.

Finch, J. 2007. "Displaying families." *Sociology* 41(1): 65–81.

Forsberg, L. 2009. *Involved parenthood. Everyday lives of Swedish middle-class families.* Ph.D. thesis, Department of Thematic Studies – Child Studies. Linköping: Linköping University.

Furedi, F. 2002. *Paranoid parenting: Why ignoring the experts may be best for your child.* Chicago: Chicago Review Press.

Gatrell, C.J. 2015. "Parenting." In *Oxford bibliographies in childhood studies,* edited by H. Montgomery. New York: Oxford University Press [online].

Gatrell, C.J., S.B. Burnett, C.L. Cooper, and P. Sparrow. 2013. "Work–life balance and parenthood: A comparative review of definitions, equity and enrichment." *International Journal of Management Reviews* 15: 300–316.

Gillies, V. 2012. "Family policy and the politics of parenting: From function to competence." In *The politicization of parenthood – shifting private and public responsibilities in education and child rearing,* edited by M. Richter, and S. Andresen, 13–26. Dordrecht: Springer.

Goodman, J. 2008. "Responding to children's needs: Amplifying the caring ethics." *Journal of Philosophy of Education* 42(2): 233–248.

Grumløse, S.P. 2014. *Den gode barndom: dansk familiepolitik 1960–2010 og forståelsen af småbarnets gode liv*. [Good childhood: Danish family policies from 1960 to 2010 and the conceptualisation of the good life for infants], Ph.D. thesis, Department of Psychology and Educational Studies. Roskilde: Roskilde University.

Hays, S. 1996. *The cultural contradictions of motherhood*. New Haven: Yale University Press.

James, A., and A. Prout, eds. 1990. *Constructing and reconstructing childhood: Contemporary issues in the sociological study of childhood*. London: Falmer.

James, A., C. Jenks, and A. Prout. 1998. *Theorizing childhood*. Cambridge: Polity Press.

Jenks, C. 1996. *Childhood*. New York: Routledge.

Law, J. 2004. *After method: Mess in social science research*. London: Routledge.

Lee, N. 1998. "Towards an immature sociology." *The Sociological Review* 46(3): 458–482.

Lee, E., J. Bristow, C. Faircloth, and J. Macvarish, eds. 2014. *Parenting culture studies*. Basingstoke: Palgrave Macmillan.

Lister, R. 2008. "Investing in children and childhood: A new welfare policy paradigm and its implications." *Comparative Social Research* 25: 383–408.

Lundqvist, Å. 2011. *Family policy paradoxes. Gender equality and labour market regulation in Sweden, 1930–2010*. Bristol: The Policy Press.

Mayall, B. 2013. *A history of the sociology of childhood*. London: IOE Press.

Morgan, D.H.J. 2011. *Rethinking family practices*. Basingstoke: Palgrave Macmillan.

Oelkers, N. 2012. The redistribution of responsibility between state and parents: Family in the context of post-welfare-state transformation. In *The politicization of parenthood – shifting private and public responsibilities in education and child rearing*, edited by M. Richter, and S. Andresen, 101–111. Dordrecht: Springer.

Prout, A. 2005. *The future of childhood. Towards the interdisciplinary study of children*. London: Routledge Falmer.

Ramaekers, S., and J. Suissa. 2012. *The claims of parenting: Reasons, responsibility and society*. Dordrecht: Springer.

Shirani, F., K. Henwood, and C. Coltart. 2012. "Meeting the challenges of intensive parenting culture: Gender, risk management and the moral parent." *Sociology* 46(1): 25–40.

Smart, C., and B. Neale. 1999. *Family fragments?* Cambridge: Polity Press.

Smith, K. 2012. "Producing governable subjects: Images of childhood old and new." *Childhood* 19(1): 24–37.

Smith, C., and S. Green. 2014. "Interview with Alan Prout." In *Key thinkers in childhood studies*, edited by C. Smith and S. Green, 169–178. Bristol: Policy Press.

UN Convention on the Rights of the Child. 1989. United Nations.

Van Blerk, L., J. Barker, N. Ansell, F. Smith, and M. Kesby. 2009. "Researching children's geographies." In *Doing children's geographies: Methodological issues*

in research with young people, edited by L. Van Blerk and M. Kesby, 1–8. London: Routledge.
Wells, M., and D. Bergnehr. 2014. "Families and family policies in Sweden." In *Handbook of family policies across the globe*, edited by M. Robila, 91–107. New York: Springer.
Westerling, A. 2015. "Reflexive fatherhood in everyday life: The case of Denmark." *Families, relationships and societies* 4(2): 209–223.
Wissö, T. 2012. *Småbarnsföräldrars vardagsliv: Omsorg, moral och socialt kapital* [Everyday life of parents of newly born: Care, moral and social capital], Ph.D. thesis, Department of Social Work, Gothenburg: University of Gothenburg.

Judith Lind, Ph.D., is Lecturer at the Department of Thematic Studies – Child Studies, Linköping University, Sweden, where she is the director of the Master's and Ph.D. programmes in Child Studies. Her general research interests concern the relationships between parents, children and the state. She is currently involved in research projects on parental support, adoption and assisted reproduction and has a particular interest in the vetting of would-be parents.

Allan Westerling, Ph.D., is Associate Professor at the Department of People & Technology, Roskilde University, Denmark. He is a member and co-founder of the Centre for Childhood, Youth and Family Life Research in this department. He is a social psychologist working across the fields of psychology and sociology. His area of research covers fatherhood, parenthood and family life. Particular interests include the institutionalisation of care under the welfare state, and the consequences of individualisation for family life.

Anna Sparrman, Ph.D., is a professor at the Department of Thematic Studies – Child Studies, Linköping University, Sweden. Her general research interests concern norms and values of children and childhood by combining visual culture, child consumption, child culture and child sexuality. She was research leader of the research project "Culture for and by Children" and has recently published *The ontological practice of child culture* together with her collaborators. Sparrman has a special interest in ethnography and visual research methods.

Karen Ida Dannesboe, Ph.D., is Assistant Professor at the Department of Educational Anthropology, School of Education, Aarhus University, Denmark. Central research areas include childhood; relations between children, family and the welfare state; materiality and identity. More specific research interests are children's everyday lives across institutions, the institutionalisation of childhood, school–family relations and parenthood.

CHAPTER 2

Time for Good Parenthood: A Study of Intercountry Adoption Assessment

Cecilia Lindgren

Abstract The aim of this study is to explore how parents' opinions and actions related to time are presented in intercountry adoption assessment reports concerning applicants who have been granted consent to adopt. As these reports establish what is required for someone to be categorised as a suitable parent, they construct and display the moral order of parenthood. An analysis of statements about time, as it relates to parental leave, working hours, preschool hours, family activities, leisure time and hobbies, illustrates how meanings of good parenthood are discursively produced. Good parents make time for, and spend time with, their children. They invest in togetherness by exchanging time of lesser value for time of greater value. This officially sanctioned understanding of good parenthood corresponds with the cultural norm of involved, devoted and child-centred parents, and reinforces the romanticised image of quality time and togetherness in the lives of nuclear families.

Keywords Intercountry adoption · Parent assessment · Family time · Morality

C. Lindgren (✉)
Department of Thematic Studies – Child Studies, Linköping University, Linköping, Sweden
e-mail: cecilia.lindgren@liu.se

© The Author(s) 2016
A. Sparrman et al. (eds.), *Doing Good Parenthood*, Palgrave Macmillan Studies in Family and Intimate Life, DOI 10.1007/978-3-319-46774-0_2

In intercountry adoption, it is the responsibility of the receiving state to guarantee that a child is placed with suitable parents (Hague Convention on the Protection of Children and Co-operation in Respect of Intercountry Adoption 1993). In Sweden, prospective adoptive parents are investigated by the social services. Based on the social worker's assessment report, including a statement on the applicants' suitability as parents, the social welfare committee decides whether or not they will be granted consent to adopt. If granted consent, applicants may proceed and have their documents forwarded to a sending country (National Board of Health and Welfare (NBHW 2009).

For an adoption to take place, the assessment report must demonstrate, to both the Swedish authorities and a child's representatives abroad, that the applicants will live up to the standard for what is perceived to be good parenthood. Consequently, it must offer information, descriptions and arguments supporting such a conclusion. Given this, adoption assessment reports constitute unique data for studying an officially sanctioned definition of good parenthood.

Norms and ideals of parenthood, childhood and family are socially reproduced in adoption policy and practice, especially in the assessment process (Modell 2002; Stryker 2010). Adopting a theoretical perspective on social work narratives, with a focus on moral accounts and categorisation (Hall 1997; Hall et al. 2006; Hydén 1997; Noordegraaf et al. 2009), I read assessment reports as narratives that construct and reconstruct the moral order of parenthood. By this, I mean that they establish, through description, what is required for someone to be categorised as a good parent. I, thus, assume that what applicants are reported to say, think and do also communicates what good parents should say, think and do, and that the narratives, thereby, display the moral order of parenthood. Therefore, the aim of this chapter is to investigate how applicants who have been granted consent to adopt are portrayed and how standards of good parenthood are formulated. It will focus on one particular aspect of the assessment, namely time.

PARENTHOOD AND THE VALUE OF TIME

In research, as well as popular culture and people's everyday lives, time is discussed as an important aspect of parenting ideals and practices. Research on family life in Sweden (Björnberg 2002; Forsberg 2009; Lindgren 2015) describes a cultural norm of involved and equal parenthood, according to which both mothers and fathers make time to care for and be together with their children. International studies also illustrate how time is crucial to ideals of parenthood. Kerry J. Daly (2001) argues that "family time" is a prescriptive term that relates to Western ideals of togetherness and child-centredness, and entails a call for parents to act in certain ways. The importance of time relies on the idea that time, and love, is what creates strong relationships between parents and their children, an idea that has been described as "a dominant cultural trope that shapes the ways in which Americans conceive of parenting" (Kremer-Sadlik and Paugh 2007, 292). In relation to adoption, time is also asserted to be important. The Swedish assessment guidelines call on social workers to investigate whether the applicants will have time for a child – time to listen, communicate, play, and read (NBHW 2009).

In today's society, however, time is said to be scarce. People experience "time squeeze" or "time famine", and parents in particular seem to feel there is never enough family time (Daly 2001; Kremer-Sadlik and Paugh 2007; Larsson 2012; Nockolds 2016; Wingard 2007). This contradiction between what parents want (time for family) and what they experience (lack of time) leads to feelings of guilt (Daly 2001; Torre 2007). This illustrates how time is valued in relation to how it is used, and that time has a moral value (Daly 1996; Fuehrer 2010). Julia Brannen states that "family life and care responsibilities are construed in relation to notions of morality" (Brannen 2005, 117); that is, to notions of how people ought to live their lives and what it means to make good use of time, and she concludes that family time and quality time are symbols of a proper family life. Ramón Torre also points to how the use of time, in everyday speech associated with children and family, "is subject to strict moral judgment indicating that what is at stake is the notion of what is good" (Torre 2007, 163–164).

Given this, the specific question to be addressed here is how time is made relevant in the categorisation of adoption applicants as suitable parents, and how descriptions related to time contribute to the construction of good parenthood.

The Study

The study is part of a research project involving the assessment of applicants for intercountry adoption in Sweden.[1] The empirical data consist of 106 assessment reports from 62 social services units in 52 municipalities.

While the assessment of first-time adoption applicants who have no biological children must focus on their potential as parents, reports on applicants who already have children also describe and evaluate their actual parenting capabilities. This study focuses on the 48 reports assessing applicants who, at the time of the assessment, had biological children or had adopted before.

Out of the 48 reports, 32 concern married couples who have no biological children but have adopted before, and 11 concern couples who have biological children. The remaining reports concern three couples in which one of the spouses has children from a previous marriage and two single women who have no biological children but have adopted before. Each report consists of 8–12 typewritten pages and includes sections on the applicants' personal background, current life situation, health status, personality and hobbies, motives for adoption and knowledge about and experience of children. It concludes with the social worker's summary and recommendations. In the following, all names have been changed to protect the identity of individuals.

The analytical focus will be on how the reports, and particularly statements related to time, construct the applicants as good parents. As Christopher Hall, Stefan Slembrouck and Srikant Sarangi point out, claiming that someone is a poor parent or, as in this case, a good parent, requires "a formulation that demonstrates her as possessing attributes and behaviours which warrant the category" (Hall et al. 2006, 22). Through an analysis of the formulations that allow for the applicants to be categorised as suitable parents, the meaning ascribed to good parenthood can be demonstrated. In the research process, all statements related to the applicants as parents were coded with a focus on time and analysed in relation to two themes: *making time for parenting* and *spending time with the children*.

MAKING TIME FOR PARENTING

In Sweden, the parents of a child are entitled to 480 days of parental leave paid by the government, to be taken during the child's first 8 years. Sixty days are reserved specifically for the mother and 60 for the father. Furthermore, parents who have used all 480 days, or want to save some of them for later, have the right to work part time to be able to spend more time with their child.

The assessment reports include information about how long the parents have stayed at home and how the time has been distributed between the spouses:

> Miranda stayed at home during the first year with both children, after which Matthew stayed at home for approximately half a year. (A32)

> Sarah and Joe took turns being on parental leave, and frequently both were at home with Theo at the same time. (A62)

Even though this is presented as relatively straightforward information, the statements effectively communicate what is desirable. When it is pointed out that both parents have stayed at home, perhaps even at the same time, that they have shared the parental leave or that they have taken turns to stay at home (e.g. A43, A56, A83), an ideal of equal engagement and responsibility is displayed.

If parents have stayed at home for an extra-long period, this is also commented upon. Dana stayed at home for 3 years, the report says, and when Toby and Martha adopted, he was at home for the first few months and then she stayed at home until their daughter turned 4 and started preschool (F12, A79). It is reported that Jessica stayed at home with her and her husband's biological son for two and a half years and now works part time. Then, the following is added: "Jessica enjoys being at work, but has chosen to be at home a great deal with Ephraim" (A100). Rhetorically, this statement accomplishes two things. It makes clear that Jessica does not stay at home because she does not like to work, or because she has problems at work. On the contrary, she enjoys her work but has chosen to stay at home. This implicitly presents her as a devoted, unselfish mother who prioritises parenthood, and being together with her child, over work.

The meaning of good parenthood that statements about parental leave produce can be illustrated with a quote from the report on a couple with two adopted children:

> After the spouses had received Joni, both took parental leave for 15 months. During this time, Nina did not attend preschool and they were all together during the day, something they describe as invaluable for the bonding process and for the children's feeling of security. (A28)

These parents have both been on parental leave, they have stayed at home for quite a long period, and they have stayed at home together, with both of their children. They have invested in togetherness. On top of this, they present arguments referring to attachment theory and professional discourse on adopted children's needs. They live up to everything that is asserted in the reports that present applicants as good parents.

At the time of the assessment, most applicants had returned to work and their children were attending preschool or school. Statements about time are, therefore, also related to working hours and preschool hours. If one or both parents are working part time, this is mentioned in the report. This communicates that parents try to minimise their working hours and maximise their time at home with their children; that is, that they make time for parenthood.

Closely connected to information about parents' working hours are statements concerning the time their children spend in preschool. Three-year-old Sam, for instance, goes to preschool 4 days a week and stays at home with his father one day, the report says (A57). Reporting that parents cut down on work so their children "will not have such long days" in preschool or "do not have to go every day" (e.g. F2, A3, A43) produces an image of parents who prioritise their children and make time to be with them. It also indicates, however, that spending too much time in preschool should be avoided. The report on 5-year-old Nick's parents says that he:

> /.../spends 15–20 hours a week in preschool. Nick's grandmother and grandfather help with Nick on a regular basis so he won't have to go to preschool every day. Nick enjoys preschool. (A37)

Even though Nick's parents work full time and cannot be at home themselves, they see to it that he can come home and that he is taken care of by his grandparents. Spending time with Grandma and Grandpa is thus considered more valuable than spending time in preschool. Reports on parents going to great lengths to minimise preschool time could of course also raise questions such as: Are they keeping their child in a preschool that is not good? Is the child uncomfortable there? In the statement above, however, the last sentence neatly rules out such a reading. Adding that "Nick enjoys preschool" makes it clear that the only reason his parents minimise his preschool time is to maximise his time at home with family. This is what good parents do.

Parents who work full time are also reported to find ways to maximise their time at home with their children. Living close to the office, being able to work from home and having flexible hours (e.g. A28, A62, A1) are presented as circumstances that make it possible for parents to keep preschool days shorter. Mary's workplace, for instance, is located close to her home, which, according to the report, "saves time when one has young children" (A56). The choice of words here is interesting since time cannot really be saved in any objective sense. It instead indicates that time is charged with moral value. Here, saving time means exchanging misused time, like commuting to and from work, for well-used time; that is, being at home taking care of your children. The report about one couple says that they both have flexible hours, "which gives them the opportunity to always prioritise the children" (A58). And the report on a single mother states that, because she usually works from home, she "is there for Zoe after preschool" (A86). Formulations like these, about saving time, being there for the child and always prioritising the children, convey the moral order of parenthood. This is how time should be used.

To summarise, statements regarding parental leave, working hours and preschool hours communicate what good parents do. They stay at home with their small children, and when returning to work they take measures to minimise working and preschool hours and maximise the time at home. They invest in togetherness and make time for parenthood. In the moral economy of time (Brannen 2005; Daly 1996; Fuehrer 2010), however, it is not only how much time one has that counts but also, as Torre (2007) points out, what one does with it.

SPENDING TIME WITH THE CHILDREN

Besides information about how applicants organise their everyday lives, the assessment reports also include descriptions of what they like to do and how they spend their time outside work. Statements related to family activities, leisure time and hobbies state that the applicants prioritise family life and being with their children (e.g. A19, A44, A91), that being together as a family with the children is the "most important" thing in their lives (e.g. A43, F2, F22), and that their children are also their "main hobby" (e.g. A11, A29, A97). For example, Richard and Leslie say, according to the report, that their best days are those spent together with their daughter (A1). Not only do these statements tell us that parents spend time with their children, they also communicate that this is what they really want to do.

It is reported that applicants spend time with their children, give them time, devote time to being with them, and fill their time with caring for them (e.g. A58, F28, F12, A83). Time devoted to being with children is also quantitatively valued, as applicants are reported to spend "a great deal of time", "most of their time" or "all of their time" together with their children (e.g. A21, A60, A82). Through such statements, the applicants are constructed as devoted and child-centred parents. They make good use of their time.

The moral value of time is also played out in statements on applicants' hobbies and leisure activities. In the reports, it is pointed out that becoming parents has been a life-changing experience for them and that they now have new priorities in life. This means that they no longer have time for their own hobbies but instead engage in activities their children choose or enjoy:

> Rose's great interest used to be sailing. Since the children came it's them, and the family, that we prioritise. (A52)

> Since our son was born there have been more walks and bike rides with him than visits to the gym. (F21)

Statements like these make it clear that parents have altered the ways in which they spend their time and effectively illustrate how time for themselves has been converted into time for their children. This, again, contributes to the construction of good parents as unselfish, devoted and willing to invest time in togetherness and family bonds.

Connected to descriptions of how parents always prioritise being with their children are comments on whether parents who are married spend time together. Formulations on this topic indicate, in very sophisticated ways, what is expected of good parents:

> As a couple they sometimes try to do something on their own (in which case both sets of grandparents help by babysitting Oliver); at these times they enjoy going to a concert or a play. (F22)

Rhetorically, several things are accomplished in this statement. The words "sometimes" and "try" tell us that these parents have an ambition to spend time together as a couple, and that they want to. It also makes clear, however, that it does not happen very often. When it does happen, their son, as the information in parentheses assures the reader, is taken care of by his grandparents. Furthermore, the mention of concerts and plays signals mutual interests and a preference for cultural activities. What is produced here is an image of good parents who enjoy each other's company and spend most of their time with their son. On the rare occasions when they do go out by themselves, they see to it that their son's time is not lost but rather invested in his relationship with extended family members.

There are also statements reporting on parents who succeed in finding time to be on their own. Kate and Ed, for example, sometimes have lunch together during workdays and are said to highly appreciate these moments (A6). The report about David and Irene tells us that, because they have established a good bedtime routine and their son goes to sleep at 7, they have the evenings to themselves (F2). Rhetorically, such reports also reinforce the image of the applicants as good parents: even though they manage to tend to their relationship, time for themselves never takes time away from their children.

To summarise, statements regarding family activities, leisure time and hobbies communicate what good parents do: they spend most of their time together with their children, engaged in child-centred activities, and they do not take time for their own personal hobbies. Good parents convert time for themselves into time for their children, not as a sacrifice but because this is what they want the most.

Concluding Discussion

The analysis of how the meaning of good parenthood is produced through description has illustrated how time related to children and parenting is charged with moral value. In assessment reports, certain ways of talking and acting in relation to time are associated with good parenting. Good parents do whatever they can to maximise their and their children's time at home; that is, they make time for parenting. When at home, they prioritise being together with their children and engage in child-centred activities; that is, they spend time with their children. Good parents hence convert time for themselves, that is time for work or hobbies, into time for their children. According to the moral order of parenthood, they exchange time of lesser value for time of greater value.

Time is a moral resource that can be invested, donated or kept to oneself, Torre (2007) argues, and in the reports, parents are described as giving and devoting time to their children. However, this donation of time is not portrayed as a sacrifice, but rather as an investment in togetherness and something that parents really want to do. Accordingly, what characterises good parenthood is epitomised by the couple who say they have had so much "us time" and now want to have "parenting time", and by the father who can sit with his son "for hours and play with cars without getting bored".

This construction of good parenthood corresponds well with the cultural norm of involved parenthood, and ideals emphasising togetherness and child-centred parenting described in previous research (Daly 2001; Forsberg 2009; Kremer-Sadlik and Paugh 2007; Lindgren 2015). It also means, however, that ideals and expectations of good parenthood that lead to parents' feelings of guilt and inadequacy are consolidated and reproduced by Swedish social service authorities in the process of assessing adoption applicants. Thus, the romanticised image of the nuclear family, in which parents and children spend quality time together, is reinforced.

Note

1. This work was supported by the Swedish Research Council (70201801) and the Swedish Research Council for Health, Working Life and Welfare (2015–00542). The research procedure was reviewed and approved by the Regional Ethical Review Board, Linköping, Sweden (3510180000).

References

Björnberg, U. 2002. "Ideology and choice between work and care." *Critical Social Policy* 22(1): 33–52.

Brannen, J. 2005. "Time and the negotiation of work-family boundaries: Autonomy or illusion?" *Time & Society* 14(1): 113–131.

Daly, K.J. 1996. *Families and time: Keeping pace in a hurried culture*. London: Sage Publications.

Daly, K.J. 2001. "Deconstructing family time: From ideology to lived experience." *Journal of Marriage and Family* 63(2): 283–294.

Forsberg, L. 2009. *Involved parenthood: Everyday lives of Swedish middle-class families*, Ph.D. thesis, Department of Thematic Studies – Child Studies, Linköping: Linköping University.

Fuehrer, P. 2010. *Om tidens värde: En sociologisk studie av senmodernitetens temporala livsvärldar*. [About the value of time: A sociological study of the temporal life worlds of late modernity], Ph.D. thesis, Department of Sociology, Stockholm: Stockholm University.

Hall, C. 1997. *Social work as narrative*. Aldershot: Ashgate.

Hall, C., S. Slembrouck, and S. Sarangi. 2006. *Language practices in social work*. London: Routledge.

Hydén, L.-C. 1997. "The institutional narrative as drama." In *The construction of professional discourse*, edited by B.-L. Gunnarsson, P. Linell, and B. Nordberg, 245–264. London: Longman.

Kremer-Sadlik, T., and A.L. Paugh. 2007. "Everyday moments: Finding 'quality time' in American working families." *Time & Society* 16(2/3): 287–308.

Larsson, J. 2012. *Studier i tidsmässig välfärd – med fokus på tidsstrategier och tidspolitik för småbarnsfamiljer*. [Studies in temporal welfare – Focusing on time strategies and time politics for families with small children], Ph.D. thesis, Department of Sociology, Göteborg: Göteborg University.

Lindgren, C. 2015. "Ideals of parenting and childhood in the contact zone of intercountry adoption: Assessment of second-time adoption applicants in Sweden." *Childhood* 22(4): 474–489.

Modell, J.S. 2002. *A sealed and secret kinship: Policies and practices in American adoption*. New York: Berghahn Books.

National Board of Health and Welfare, NBHW. 2009. *Adoption: Handbook for the Swedish social services*. Stockholm: Socialstyrelsen.

Nockolds, D. 2016. "Acceleration for working sole parents: Squeezed between institutional temporalities and routinized parenting practices." *Time & Society* 25(3): 513–532.

Noordegraaf, M., C. Van Nijnatten, and E. Elbers. 2009. "Assessing candidates for adoptive parenthood." *Children and Youth Services Review* 31: 89–96.

Stryker, R. 2010. *The road to Evergreen: Adoption, attachment therapy, and the promise of family*. Ithaca: Cornell University Press.

Torre, R.R. 2007. "Time's social metaphors." *Time & Society* 16(2/3): 157–187.

Wingard, L. 2007. "Constructing time and prioritizing activities in parent-child interaction." *Discourse & Society* 18(1): 75–91.

Cecilia Lindgren, Ph.D., is an associate professor at the Department of Thematic Studies – Child Studies, Linköping University, Sweden. Her research interests include the history of family and childhood, child adoption policy and practices, and child politics in the Nordic welfare states. Her most recent work is on the assessment of parenting capacity in social services.

CHAPTER 3

No One of Importance: Lesbian Mothers' Constructions of Permanently Anonymous Sperm Donors

Anna Malmquist, Anna Polski and Karin Zetterqvist Nelson

Abstract The present study discusses how Swedish lesbian couples argue for their choice of permanently anonymous donors after conceiving at fertility clinics in Denmark. In a Swedish context, these women challenge both the established Swedish practice of identity-release donors *and* the previously common practice of lesbian mothers engaging in joint parenthood with gay fathers. Altogether 78 mothers have been interviewed. Discourse analysis show that the interviewees use two main constructions when talking about the permanently anonymous sperm donor: "the donor is not a father" and "the donor is the child's other half". The study shows how both these constructions serve to justify that the mothers are good parents. Central aspects in doing good parenthood is to have a close

A. Malmquist (✉)
Department of Behavioural Sciences and Learning, Linköping University,
Linköping, Sweden
e-mail: anna.malmquist@liu.se

A. Polski
Department of Psychology, Lund University, Lund, Sweden

K. Zetterqvist Nelson
Department of Thematic Studies – Child Studies, Linköping University,
Linköping, Sweden

© The Author(s) 2016
A. Sparrman et al. (eds.), *Doing Good Parenthood*, Palgrave Macmillan
Studies in Family and Intimate Life, DOI 10.1007/978-3-319-46774-0_3

parent–child relationship, taking care of the child in everyday life and acknowledge the child's future search for its identity.

Keywords Lesbian couples · Fatherhood · Motherhood · Anonymous sperm donor · Discourse analysis

Lesbian women who decide to have children together find several different pathways to parenthood. They may choose to cooperate with men who give them sperm for self-insemination. Some also choose to share daily parenting with this man once the child is born. Two women may also have fertility treatment at a clinic, adopt or have foster children. In Sweden, women in lesbian relations have only had access to fertility treatment since 2005 (Proposition 2004/2005:137). Until recently, it was common for Swedish lesbian couples to turn to gay men for shared parenting arrangements in two households (Ryan-Flood 2009; Zetterqvist Nelson 2007). More recently however, a shift seems to have taken place in Swedish lesbians' preferred paths to parenthood, as turning to fertility clinics has become more common (Malmquist 2015a). Since lesbians gained access to public fertility clinics in Sweden, utilizing these clinics' services has been established as a common path to parenthood. Turning to private fertility clinics in Denmark is also common among Swedish lesbians.

The cultural understanding of sperm donation has undergone vast changes during recent decades (Daniels 2007). Previously, anonymous donation was seen as a natural way of protecting both the donor and the (heterosexual) parents, in a context where infertility and donation were generally kept a secret from people in the parents' surroundings – including the offspring. Lately, genetic heritage has been attributed greater value in Western societies, and sperm donors' status has changed: they are construed as the child's biogenetic origin, and in that regard are seen as crucial to the child's identity development (Cowden 2012; Turkmendag et al. 2008). Adhering to such a discourse, Swedish clinics only allow identity-release donors in fertility treatments, that is, where offspring, once mature, are allowed obtain full information on the donor's identity (Isaksson et al. 2011). In Denmark, in contrast, donors are generally permanently anonymous, even though identity-release donor semen currently is an option at Danish clinics as well (Ernst et al. 2007). Lesbian women's choice to turn to either a Swedish or Danish fertility clinic is affected by a number of different circumstances (cf. Malmquist and Zetterqvist Nelson 2014; Rozental and Malmquist 2015), where the preference for either an identity-release donor or an anonymous donor is one factor they have to take into account.

In the present chapter, we will scrutinize how Swedish lesbian couples argue for their choice of permanently anonymous donors, after conceiving at fertility clinics in Denmark. In a Swedish context, these women challenge both the established Swedish practice of identity-release donors *and* the previously common practice of lesbian mothers engaging in joint parenthood with gay fathers. We will show how their accounts reflect different ways of talking about sperm donors, which in turn, reveals how the mothers construe good parenthood. As the present chapter will show, central aspects of their construction of the good parent include a close parent–child relationship and parents' taking care of the child in everyday life; parents also acknowledge the child's future search for its identity.

THE STUDY

The present chapter is part of a larger interview study on lesbian motherhood in Sweden (see Malmquist 2016, 2015a, b, c; Malmquist et al. 2014; Malmquist and Zetterqvist Nelson 2014; Rozental and Malmquist 2015). In this study, 96 women in 51 lesbian families have been interviewed by Anna Malmquist in 2009 and 2010 (cf. Malmquist 2015a for an extensive description of the participants and data collection). The semi-structured interviews follow an interview guide that invite the participants to reflect over their paths to parenthood and experiences of parenting. Most of the interviewees have utilized permanently anonymous donors in Denmark, and the meaning of this choice is discussed in 35 interviews with 67 mothers. These 35 interviews are analysed in this chapter. In 2012, seven additional interviews with 11 mothers in seven families were carried out by Anna Polski, the aim being to obtain focused and in-depth interview data on the meaning of utilizing permanently anonymous donors. An interview guide that focuses specifically on the choice of anonymous donors was developed for those interviews (see Polski 2013 for a comprehensive description of the data collection and participants). The analysis was initially conducted on the data generated from the seven interviews with a specific focus on donation and with a theoretical Foucauldian discourse analytical approach (Willig 2008). Such analysis is concerned with identifying and describing the different discourses available in a specific context, as well as the power resources relating to them. The analysis also pays attention to the effect that discourse has on the subject in focus. In the second step, the selection of interview segments from the first study (35 interviews) were added to the analysis made by Polski (2013). This chapter presents findings from both datasets. All in all, the chapter covers interviews with 78 mothers in 42 families. When quoted in the results section, all interviewees and their children have been given pseudonyms.

The majority of the interviewees describe their chosen path to parenthood as being preferable to other options. They depict shared parenting with a man or two men as being too complicated, and claim that they wanted to build their family on their own. A few interviewees, however, state that they would have preferred an involved father, or at least an identity-release donor, but anonymous donor semen had been chosen because this was accessible for them. Most interviewees talk about the person who anonymously contributed the semen as the donor, while one couple recurrently refers to the anonymous donor as the father. Two main constructions of the donor were found in the interviews and labelled *the donor is not a father* and *the donor is the other half*. Most interviewees draw on both constructions in different ways, depending on the topic and conversational context, despite their contradictory meanings. In the following, each construction is presented separately, and in relation to each construction we discuss the associated discourses and what the interviewees gain from the construction.

The Donor Is Not a Father

When talking about the donor, most interviewees spontaneously state that the donor is not a father, or that the donor is not a parent. The interviewee Petra makes such claim:

> Because we've been careful to stress that they don't have a **father**,[1] they have a donor, that's a completely different thing, but they don't have a father because at least I think, well we both do really, that a father plays an active role, if he's called a father.

Petra explicitly states that the donor is not a father; a donor is "a completely different thing". She also provides a definition of a father, as she claims that a father plays an "active role". This way of clearly stating that a donor is not a father is common in the interviews. Several interviewees also state that "**we** are the parents", in contrast to the donor who is not a parent. The interviewees' ways of spontaneously and explicitly stating that the donor is not a father could be understood in relation to a predominating discourse in which the donor *is* construed as a father. In a heteronormative context, where it is considered self-evident that every child has a mother and a father, the donor is recurrently referred to as a father. Such a discourse is identifiable in the interviewees' stories about how others tend to talk about the donor as being a father. In the following, Sofie describes how she and her partner have engaged in such a dialogue with the child's preschool teacher.

> Once again we had to go to school and explain to her how Oliver was conceived, through insemination, and that there was no father in the picture at all, **at all**, but an anonymous donor, and that was our conscious choice, and then her reaction, her personal opinion, came into it, "yes but all children have the right to search for their parents, their mother and their father and everything".

Sofie presents as a fact that her son Oliver was conceived "through insemination" and therefore does not have a father "at all". She thereby draws a sharp line between a father and "an anonymous donor". The teacher, on the other hand, according to Sofie, talks about donors as "their parents", "their mother and their father" and as someone the child has a right to "search for". The image of the donor as a father could also be understood in relation to a discourse in which genetic bonds define kinship. Several interviewees make claims that disqualify such a discourse, stating that parenthood is something different from biology or genetics. A parent is depicted as someone who is "present in everyday life", someone who has a "relation" to the child, who "plays, reads stories", who do parenthood. Interviewee Katta claims that parents are "the people who've raised her, who've been there, who've given her security and love, that's what defines your parents". Based on such a definition of parenthood, an anonymous donor is clearly not a parent. Rather, the account serves to show that the lesbian couple are the parents, doing good parenthood by nurturing the child in the family's everyday life.

In relation to claiming that the donor is not a father or a parent, several interviewees also talk about what the donor *is*. The donor is commonly depicted as a helper, that is someone who is kind and generous. Ellen talks about the donor as a helper.

> And furthermore we, Jessica and I, **are** the parents, and we don't want him to think he has another parent, you know. That's why we chose well, not to get, or have open [donation]. Because we feel that we, **we're** the parents and the donor is just a kind man who helped us out.

According to Ellen, the donor is "just" a helpful and kind man, and not "another parent". Here, Ellen claims to have chosen a permanently anonymous donor so that her son would not "think" that he has another parent somewhere. In this way, the construction of the donor as a helper functions to strengthen the picture of the donor as a non-parent. Another way of presenting the donor as a non-parent is to claim that the donor is "no one of importance", not anyone they are "interested in". Interviewee Rakel says: "To me it doesn't matter, I mean they're my children, it doesn't matter who, who donated". Several interviewees also stress that it is "just sperm" that someone has given, in a way that rhetorically minimizes the meaning and impact of the donor.

Throughout the interview data, it is clear that it is important for the interviewees to establish that the donor is not a father or a parent, and that his impact is limited. But why is this so important? What is at stake for them? We argue that this rhetorical work entails two important gains for the interviewees. First, when the meaning of the donor is minimized, the child is presented in a way that clarifies that s/he is not missing out on anything significant by not having a relation to the donor. Second, when parenthood is bound to social relations rather than biology, the position of the non-birth mother is rhetorically strengthened. This is how the parents account for themselves as good parents. Interviewee Edda's first child was conceived at a Danish clinic, utilizing an anonymous donor. When they desired a second child, she and her partner turned to a Swedish clinic, where only identity-release donors are allowed. In the following excerpt, Edda describes her reaction when a staff member at the Swedish clinic claimed that the older child would later develop problems because the donor was anonymous:

> Not that I get upset so often, what other people think doesn't matter, but. So afterward, I said to her "No, I don't think so, actually, because we talk

with her [their daughter] all the time and she knows the situation and it doesn't matter". When you talk to the child, they have two parents and a huge family, around the child, they have support. Heredity doesn't matter, at least that's what I think. And the idea that you can knock on a stranger's door and that, that you, what's that about?

When describing how she was criticized for utilizing an anonymous donor, Edda argues strongly to defend her choice. The donor is rhetorically minimized to "a stranger", and it is claimed that "heredity doesn't matter". Rather, Edda emphasizes the importance of the present "two parents and a huge family". Clearly, minimizing the impact of the donor and emphasizing the importance of the mothers' function constitute a way of defending the lesbian family structure. Edda defends herself and her partner by claiming that they are fully sufficient parents on their own; they are good parents.

The Donor Is the Child's Other Half

Besides talking about the donor as a non-father, several interviewees also construe the donor as the child's other half. The donor is discussed in terms of "genetic origins", "biological inheritance", "roots", "background" and "biological father". All such statements give the donor recognition and an impact, which would seem to contradict the above-described construction of the donor as unimportant. Several parents discuss how they can imagine the children possibly having thoughts about the donor when forming their own identities as teenagers. Lotta and Mikaela discuss this issue in their interview.

> *Lotta*:   So they **will** wonder, of course, when they get older, I think they will, it's natural, why am I like I am (*Interviewer*: yes)
> *Mikaela*:   Why do I look like I do (*Lotta*: yes) (Interviewer: yes), who was it, where is my other half, when they get big enough, it feels sort of hard really, that we've decided they'll never get to know.

Lotta and Mikaela depict it as something "natural" that people wonder about their "other half" and "why I look like I do". When referring to the donor as the children's other half, they construe the donor as part of the children. The point of departure for such a construction is that genetics is fundamental to a person's appearance and identity, and that an identity is generally something people search for. The mothers' talk adheres to a discourse in which genetic origins are an important part of identity development, and the mothers position themselves as adults who have made a "hard" decision for their children when they chose to utilize a permanently anonymous donor. Several interviewees describe their choice in terms of potentially being "egotistical", "selfish" or "unfair", and some of them state that they would have chosen an identity-release donor if that had been available at a lower price at the clinic. Typically, however, the parents justify their choice of an anonymous donor by claiming that their child will probably not have an interest in the donor anyway, or that children are usually happy with any choice the parents are comfortable with. Through such claims, the parents rhetorically minimize potential negative aspects of anonymous donation, which in turn, accounts for their choices as responsible and good parents.

Besides construing the donor as the child's other half with respect to identity development, several interviewees draw on such a construction when describing their choice of utilizing the same donor for two siblings. Most parents with two children have used the same donor, or say that they would have wanted to do so if the same donor had been available. This is generally claimed to give the children something "in common" or "the same prerequisites". Gina reflects on this choice.

> To me it's about the fact that we've **cut** half of their biological bonds, so it's just like, well giving something back to them, in some way, that at least they have the cut bonds, they have them (*Amie*, her partner: together). Yeah. In theory, really I feel like that it feels like, well it makes me blush a bit, but that's how I feel somehow. But today I can also feel that it's nice that they're a bit alike.

According to Gina, utilizing a permanently anonymous donor means that they have "cut half of their biological bonds", and utilizing the same donor for both children is a way of compensating for this, to give them something "together". Despite her strong rhetoric, she also claims that her feelings make her "blush", which points at the ideological and moral dilemma that emerges in relation to the construction of the donor as the child's other half. On the one hand, construing biological origin as important adheres to a predominating discourse on children's identity and development, which underpins an ideal of good parenthood. On the other hand, the choice of a permanently anonymous donor favours their family form, because when genetic origins are construed as inessential, this provides a space and status for both mothers – irrespective of biogenetic origin. The dilemma emerges in another interviewee's story. Non-birth mother Isabelle claims that her partner's desire to utilize the same donor for both siblings felt like an "insult to me", because if shared genetics bonds are considered important, then her function and impact as a non-genetic parent are called into question. This shows how problematic the construction of the donor as the child's other half is for parents in lesbian relations, where normative ideas about the "crucial" nature of genetic origins challenge the foundation of their family.

CONCLUDING DISCUSSION

The present analysis shows two main constructions of the permanently anonymous sperm donor: *the donor is not a father* and *the donor is the child's other half* and how both these constructions serve to justify the mothers as "good parents".

Construing the donor as a non-father has two main advantages for the interviewees. First, in a context where fatherhood is considered important, it is generally viewed as inadequate for children to have a poor or no relation to their father. When a donor is construed as an absent father, the child seems to be missing out on something crucial. Construing the donor as a non-father is therefore central when justifying the choice of an anonymous donor: the child has not lost anything, because a donor is not a father. This also explains why, in direct relation to claims that the donor is not a father, the interviewees point out that they are the child's parents. These statements serve to show that the child is being well cared for by his/her present and nurturing parents. Second, by claiming that parenthood is a matter of caretaking rather than genetics, the non-birth mother's status as the child's parent is rhetorically defended. Previous studies have shown that non-birth mothers are often seen as less of a parent, and utilizing an anonymous donor is often chosen in order to strengthen her position (Chabot and Ames 2004; Donovan and Wilson 2008; Nordqvist 2012). The construction of the donor as a non-father rhetorically ensures the child two good parents, the present and loving mothers, because parenthood is a matter of shared caretaking. It also illustrates that good parenthood is done in practice.

The second main construction, where the donor is depicted as the child's other half, also serves to justify the interviewees' doing good parenthood. This construction adheres to a discourse in which genetic origins are seen as important to a young person's identity development. When the mothers draw on such a construction, they show that they are reflecting parents who acknowledge and care about their children's potential future dilemmas. As good parents, they adhere to the normative concerns that are raised about children in lesbian families. At the same time, such concerns are rhetorically minimized as the parents account for their decisions. Here, good parenthood is done both within the parents' accounts of their decisions, and when they acknowledge the possible negative consequences of these decisions.

Note

1. Bold in the transcribed interview data marks emphasis

References

Chabot, J.M., and B.D. Ames. 2004. "It wasn't 'let's get pregnant and go do it': Decision making in lesbian couples planning motherhood via donor insemination." *Family Relations* 53(4): 348–356.

Cowden, M. 2012. "'No harm no foul': A child's right to know their genetic parents." *International Journal of Law, Policy and the Family* 26(1): 102–126.

Daniels, K. 2007. "Donor gametes: Anonymous or identified?" *Best Practice & Research Clinical Obstetrics and Gynaecology* 21(1): 113–128.

Donovan, C., and A.R. Wilson. 2008. "Imagination and integrity: Decision-making among lesbian couples to use medically provided donor insemination." *Culture, Health & Sexuality* 10(7): 649–665.

Ernst, E., H.J. Ingerslev, O. Schou, and M. Stoltenberg. 2007. "Attitudes among sperm donors in 1992 and 2002: A Danish questionnaire survey." *Acta Obstetricia et Gynecologica Scandinavica* 86(3): 327–333.

Isaksson, S., A. Skoog Svanberg, G. Sydsjö, A. Thurin-Kjellberg, and P-O. Karlström. 2011. "Two decades after legislation on identifiable donors in Sweden: Are recipient couples ready to be open about using gamete donation?" N-G *Human Reproduction* 26(4): 853–860.

Malmquist, A. 2015a. *Pride and prejudice: Lesbian families in contemporary Sweden*, Ph.D. thesis, Department of Behavioural Sciences and Learning. Linköping: Linköping University.

Malmquist, A. 2015b. "A crucial but strenuous process: Female same-sex couples' reflections on second-parent adoption." *Journal of GLBT Family Studies* 11(4): 351–374.

Malmquist, A. 2015c. "Women in lesbian relations: Construing equal or unequal parental roles?" *Psychology of Women Quarterly* 39(2): 256–267.

Malmquist, A. 2016. "'But wait where should I be, am I Mum or Dad?' Lesbian couples reflect on heteronormativity in regular antenatal education and the benefits of LGBTQ-certified options." *International Journal of Birth and Parent Education* 3(3): 7–10.

Malmquist, A., and K. Zetterqvist Nelson. 2014. "Efforts to maintain a 'just great' story: Lesbian parents' talk about encounters with professionals in fertility clinics and maternal and child health care services." *Feminism & Psychology* 24(1): 56–73.

Malmquist, A., A. Möllerstrand, M. Wikström, and K. Zetterqvist Nelson. 2014. "'A daddy is the same as a mummy': Swedish children in lesbian households talk about fathers and donors". *Childhood* 21(1): 119–133.

Nordqvist, P. 2012. "Origins and originators: Lesbian couples negotiating parental identities and sperm donor conception." *Culture, Health & Sexuality* 14(3): 297–311.

Polski, A. 2013. *Ingen av betydelse: Mödrar från samkönad familjebildning talar om spermadonatorn.* Master's thesis, Department of Psychology. Lund: Lund University.

Proposition 2004/2005:137. Assisterad befruktning och föräldraskap.

Rozental, A., and A. Malmquist. 2015. "Vulnerability and acceptance: Lesbian women's family-making through assisted reproduction in Swedish health care". *Journal of GLBT Family Studies* 11(2): 127–150.

Ryan-Flood, R. 2009. *Lesbian motherhood: Gender, families and sexual citizenship.* Basingstoke: Palgrave Macmillan.

Turkmendag, I., R. Dingwall, and T. Murphy. 2008. "The removal of donor anonymity in the UK: The silencing of claims by would-be parents." *International Journal of Law, Policy and the Family* 22: 283–310.

Willig, C. 2008. *Introducing qualitative research in psychology: Adventures in theory and method.* Buckingham: Open University Press.

Zetterqvist Nelson, K. 2007. *Mot alla odds: Regnbågsföräldrars berättelser om att bilda familj och få barn* [Against all odds: Rainbow families' narratives on starting families and have children]. Malmö: Liber.

Anna Malmquist, Ph.D., is a lecturer and researcher at the Department of Behavioural Sciences and Learning, Linköping University, Sweden. She is a social psychologist with a research interest in gender and sexuality. Her research mainly concerns same-sex parenting. In her doctoral thesis (2015), she explores conditions for lesbian mothers in contemporary Sweden.

Anna Polski has an MA and a Diploma in Psychology from the Department of Psychology, Lund University, Sweden. Polski currently works as a psychologist in Gothenburg.

Karin Zetterqvist Nelson, Ph.D., is a professor at the interdisciplinary Department of Thematic Studies – Child Studies, Linköping University, Sweden. Zetterqvist Nelson has published a number of articles about gay and lesbian parenthood, including a book in Swedish *Mot alla odds: Regnbågsföräldrars berättelser om att bilda familj och få barn* (2007). Her research interests also include the historical development of child psychology and child psychiatry in Sweden during the twentieth century.

CHAPTER 4

Parenting on the Edge: Doing Good Parenthood in Child Protection Services Interventions

Pernille Juhl

Abstract This chapter presents an analysis of parents' perspectives on good parenthood when subject to interventions from the Danish Child Protection Services. It is based on a qualitative, empirical data. The aim is to explore how parents process instructions from professionals regarding, for example, their child's health and daily routines, and what such instructions mean to parents in their daily lives. The professionals' instructions are analysed as intertwined with the complex everyday life of the children and parents. Parenthood is conceptualised as a social practice, embedded in societal structures. This means that it is the daily parental activities in the home and daily tasks in relation to supporting children's participation in other life contexts (e.g. day care) that are explored and analysed.

Keywords Child protection services · Intervention · Children's perspective · Parenthood · Everyday life

P. Juhl (✉)
Center for Childhood, Youth & Family Research, Department of People &
Technology, Roskilde University, Roskilde, Denmark
e-mail: peju@ruc.dk

© The Author(s) 2016
A. Sparrman et al. (eds.), *Doing Good Parenthood*, Palgrave Macmillan
Studies in Family and Intimate Life, DOI 10.1007/978-3-319-46774-0_4

The purpose of this chapter is to investigate parenthood in marginalised families. Specifically, I conduct a qualitative empirical study in families where the children's development and well-being are considered to be at risk by the Danish Child Protection Services (CPS). The local authorities provide social interventions (e.g. family counselling and relief families), and I explore the implicit and explicit norms and ideals of parenthood encompassed in those interventions as manifested through instructions and supervision provided by the professionals. I focus on the parents' perspectives on how the professionals' instructions have practical consequences for the family's everyday lives and how the instructions become meaningful. I draw on an understanding of family life as an activity requiring ongoing negotiations (Finch 2007; Morgan 1996). I also understand family as a social practice connected to other practices (Dreier 2008). In Denmark, family members generally spend part of their everyday lives in separate places (e.g. in day care or at work), with the family reuniting in the afternoon (Kousholt 2011). This means that children and parents live complex everyday lives. In relation to this context for family life, parenthood involves taking care of children in collaboration with professionals in shared care arrangements (Andenæs 2011; Singer 1993) and hooking up (Marschall 2013) with professionals' contributions to the care arrangement (Ulvik 2007). For parents, subject to CPS interventions, another dimension is added to the complexity of parenthood as it involves working with CPS professionals and receiving instructions on how to do good parenting. A variety of studies examine this issue. Research shows that parents involved in CPS interventions experience that the generalised knowledge of the profession has a higher status than the parents' everyday life perspectives, but that they struggle to execute CPS' instructions (Hennum 2014). Other studies show how parents try to play the game by feigning cooperation (Dumbrill 2006) and that they often feel misunderstood by social workers (Corby et al. 1996).

Based on some of the issues brought forward in the above-mentioned studies, I address two main points in this chapter. First, I argue that being a good parent cannot be understood as delimited to care activities in the home. Second, I analyse how an important co-constituent condition for parents who are subject to CPS interventions is the multi-faceted nature of the instructions about such different aspects as health promotion, child nurturing, daily routines in the family and adequate response to children's needs which professionals give. These instructions become yet another part of the opportunities available for doing good parenting (Hennum 2014).

The Study

The analysis is based on empirical data from a qualitative research project on child protection (Juhl 2014). The research design was based on ethnographic methodologies (see for instance Daly and Dienhart 1998; Hammersly and Atkinsson 2007). The analysis draws on cultural–historical traditions conceptualising the person–world relationship as dialectic and subjectivity as related to the subjects' participation in and across social practices (Andenæs 2012; Dreier 2008; Haavind 2011; Holzkamp 2013). I focus on the parents' perspectives on the opportunities and dilemmas that arise in parenting. Their personal perspectives contribute by illustrating parenthood in specific situations where parents are involved in CPS interventions. At the same time, these perspectives emphasise general conditions for parenthood in the Danish welfare state. The empirical data highlighted in this chapter presents some general dilemmas described by the parents participating in the study.

The study involved participant observations (Højholt and Kousholt 2014) of six children aged 0–4 years in the children's different life contexts such as day care and family life. I also conducted interviews with eight parents about how their everyday lives are organised and the problems they experience. Moreover, I conducted interviews with professionals from CPS as well as childminders. The study focuses on how various life conditions in a variety of life contexts interact in complex ways as analysed from the children's perspectives.

The General Context for Exploring Parenthood: The Danish Welfare State

As part of a health promotion and prevention approach, every new born child in Denmark is enrolled in the health visitor programme, which includes several routine home visits from the child's birth to age 3. The health visitor supervises the developmental well-being and health of the child. If the health visitor has concerns about the parents' or the child's behaviour or appearance, the health visitor is obliged to report the concerns to a CPS social worker, who will determine whether or not it is necessary to proceed with an investigation. If it is, the parents' parenting abilities will be scrutinised. The local authorities in Denmark provide a large number of preventive interventions that can be set in motion if a child's well-being is deemed to be at risk. An example of an intervention is more visits from the health visitor or having the mother take part in a group for vulnerable mothers that receives regular supervision by a social worker and a health visitor.

Most parents in Denmark have paid parental leave for the first year of the child's life. At the age of 1 year, the majority of children attend state-subsidised day care centres. Parenthood, therefore, implies being part of a shared care arrangement (Andenæs 2011; Singer 1993). When children and parents spend part of their day in separate places (in day care and at work), the family members reunite at the end of the day and the parents take over the care tasks and responsibility the day care professionals had during the day. Hence, caring tasks and parental responsibility are not limited to the home and family life but also include other contexts outside the parents' presence. In the following sections, I analyse what this context for doing parenthood means for parents whose children are defined as being at risk. Using empirical evidence, I illustrate how two parents, Sarah and Ben, experience the instructions they receive from CPS professionals as conflicting and contradictory when it comes to making their everyday life work.

PROFESSIONALS' CONCERNS

Sarah and Ben's son Adam is 18 months old and when he was a new born, the local health visitor came for a routine visit. In an interview I did, the health visitor explains that she was somewhat concerned because the parents did not appear to be very familiar with how to take care of an infant. For instance, the parents did not dress Adam properly according to the weather, and they generally seemed unaware of Adam's needs. Another issue of concern was the parents' history of growing up in foster care as children. The social worker was worried about whether the parents' own experiences meant that they lacked basic parenting skills. Due to these concerns, a CPS social worker got involved and suggested that the mother attend a mothers' group for vulnerable mothers as a preventive social intervention.

The parents reluctantly accepted. When I interviewed Sarah and Ben, they explained that they both find everyday life difficult, especially because Ben suffers from a chronic disease that often prevents him from taking part in care for Adam or doing domestic chores. Sometimes Ben is admitted to the hospital for weeks, leaving Sarah with primary responsibility for every-thing in the home while simultaneously trying to keep up with her studies. When Ben is doing well, most of his energy goes into his work to make up for his high level of absenteeism. When Ben is doing poorly, he and Sarah frequently fight about the care tasks and domestic chores.

When I interviewed the social worker and the health visitor, they discussed how they think that Ben and Sarah are disorganised and incapable of giving Adam a stable, everyday routine.

> Social Worker: We emphasised how Adam needs stability and predictability [...] One issue is his sleeping pattern. We have reason to believe that the parents put Adam to bed too late in the evening and that means that he is exceptionally tired the next day in the day care.

Adams' needs are used as an argument for instructing the parents to ensure stability and predictability. By presenting these concerns and giving instructions, the social worker contributes to good parenthood from a certain perspective. This perspective included ensuring healthy sleeping patterns and being able to maintain a stable routine for Adam. The professional's concern for instability in Adam's life is based on an abstract and universal understanding of children's needs (Woodhead 1991). In an attempt to establish this stability, the professionals instruct the parents to make sure that Adam only naps one time in the middle of the day and that he is put to bed around 7:30 or 8:00 p.m. every night.

Other instructions are directed at Sarah and Adam's emotional contact. Sarah is told, for example, to respond immediately when Adam cries. The professionals explain that Sarah needs to be a secure base for Adam, which can be achieved by responding appropriately to his every need. The social worker registers whether Sarah comforts Adam when he falls, whether Sarah is capable of verbally expressing what she thinks Adam is trying to tell her when he cries, and if Sarah gives Adam a large amount of physical contact and caressing.

The local authority's description of CPS interventions towards vulnerable families emphasises how:

> The level of concern must be high. We are dealing with children aged 0–3 years at risk of being placed in foster care. There is a need for special support to parents (mother) and child. Parents (mother) should be prepared to work with their lack of skills.[1]

Parenting primarily appears to involve the mother and her practices, recognised by the professionals as falling under the category of secure attachment. Fathers are not specifically referred to or included in the same way in the interventions. This is striking since Danish fathers are involved in parenting in general (Nielsen and Westerling 2015). The professionals consider it an extra but unexpected bonus if fathers contribute positively to their children's well-being. The mother is regarded as the most important person in a young child's life and the interventions and instructions are aimed at how she should act in relation to her child. In Adam's case, Ben is not considered a stable resource because of his disease but is included in the instructions on doing good parenting.

Instructions and Everyday Life as Contradictions

When I interviewed Sarah and Ben about what they thought about being subject to CPS interventions, Sarah explains:

> Sarah: It's really difficult because they [the social worker and the health visitor] urged us to have a stable pattern. We had to try to eat at the same time every evening and keep to a bedtime schedule for Adam.
> I think they [the professionals] have some kind of standard formula for how everyday life should be conducted and when to do this and that, but you know what, that just doesn't go very well together with our working hours and the whole situation with Ben's disease and Adam's mood.

Sarah explains how she finds the instructions contradictory because the family's situation is not the same every day, which presents a problem as the professionals' instruct them to maintain the same daily routine. Ben does not feel that he is involved in the interventions, stating: "It's only about Sarah and Adam . . . I don't have a say . . . " Sarah agrees with him and expresses her frustration because, from her perspective, the main problems in the family involve making ends meet when it comes to work hours, studying and picking Adam up at day care, all of which is compounded by the fact that knowing when and what Ben can help with is unpredictable. Ben, on the other hand, finds it difficult to be included in the family when he is doing well and able and willing to contribute to care tasks and household duties. The fact that the interventions are directed at Sarah and Adam only appears to reinforce the difficulties and dilemmas that challenge Ben and Sarah as collaborators working to share the responsibility for parenting.

The following example derives from my observation field notes. It is afternoon and the setting is Ben and Sarah's home. Sarah has recently picked up Adam from day care and has returned home, where Ben was waiting. Ben, feeling poorly after recently coming home from the hospital, is still tired and easily becomes annoyed when Adam cries. Ben describes how he withdraws from the family activities when he is doing poorly.

The day care worker has talked to Sarah about how Adam seemed particularly tired from the beginning of the day, which is why an exception was made and Adam was put to bed for an extra nap. Sarah told the day care worker that Adam is still suffering from a cold and that he had been awake several times during the night. Sarah learned that Adam had not been sleeping as long as usual during the day, despite the extra nap. During my visit, Sarah tells me that Adam seems more tired than usual at this time. The following excerpt from my field notes provides an example of what type of afternoon Sarah and Ben experience at home at that time:

> 5:20 pm: Adam starts to whine and rubs his eyes. Sarah takes him up on her arm, but he protests by squirming and screaming. He throws himself back and Sarah puts him down. She fetches a small pack of raisins and this seems to calm him down. His crying subsides. Sarah returns to the kitchen and starts peeling potatoes. A few minutes later, Adam starts to cry again and throws the rest of the raisins on the floor. Sarah makes several attempts to get Adam to calm down. For example, she tries to draw his attention towards the television and she fetches water and toys, but nothing seems to work. Sarah looks bewildered and asks Ben if he can start to peel the potatoes, so she can take care of Adam. Ben nods but is immersed in the computer.

Usually Adam likes to play with some plastic boxes on the kitchen floor while Sarah is cooking. But when Adam is tired, like today, he does not want to do any of these things. Occasionally, he sits in the living room watching television with Ben. Sarah tries in various ways to comfort Adam and at the same time she is keen to get dinner ready. Adam seems to be both tired and hungry at the same time. By delaying the cooking for the purpose of comforting Adam, it becomes difficult to meet Adam's urgent need for food so that he can be put to bed. This illustrates how caring for Adam is a complex and antagonistic process that requires constant prioritisation of concerns and needs. The situation constitutes a conflict between prioritising comforting Adam or preparing dinner. Whenever Sarah turns her attention to the cooking, Adam cries, and when she comforts him, the dinner is delayed. My field notes describe Sarah considering her options: "Sarah looks at the clock [nearly 5:30 pm]. 'You can't be allowed to sleep now. It's too late for a nap', she says to Adam while carrying him around trying to console him." The professionals' guidelines and directions about responding immediately to Adam's needs, regular sleep routines and nurturing fail to take into account the contradictory concerns and Adam's changing and simultaneous needs. Well-being and children's needs are not static concepts that can be supported by doing the same thing every day or by stringently following instructions.

Later that night, Sarah explains to me how, in the situation in question, she is well aware that Adam is crying because he is tired and that what he needs most of all is sleep. Yet, Sarah does not consider putting him to bed an option, stating:

> Sarah: Some nights are just really difficult when Adam is tired and he cries. Then it's not as easy as they [the CPS professionals] make it sound to just keep doing the same thing over and over! [...] Even when Adam isn't tired, then we come home late in the afternoon, and then it gets late until dinner is ready...too late according to them. If Ben hasn't had the energy to peel potatoes or...yeah, you know, just prepare the dinner or something...then it's quite difficult to eat as early as they claim is best for Adam...but, you know, I try because I'm afraid what will happen if we don't follow their instructions.

This example emphasises two issues. First, Adam's needs and well-being cannot be understood merely in relation to what is going on in the family and what the parents do. In the above situation, Adam's need for sleep in the afternoon, when he is together with his parents, is different than usual because of a shorter nap during the day. The specific care tasks, Adam's needs and the related dilemmas experienced by the parents are connected to what happened earlier in the day and in other contexts of Adam's life. This suggests that parental care connects to and builds on the care that others provide at other times and in other places. Second, I want to point out how this shared care arrangement is a common condition for parenthood and becomes particularly difficult for Adam's parents because of the social worker's narrow focus on parental care. This focus does not take into consideration how the dilemmas and Adam's concrete needs evolve situated in and in relation to his participation in and across different life contexts. What happens in other contexts influences the problems, needs and concerns that emerge at home. CPS' concerns about the parents' ability to take care of Adam mean that the parents do not feel they have permission to adjust their daily routines in accordance to how they perceive Adam's changing needs and the whole situation.

Instructions given beforehand about children's needs fail to take a changing and complex everyday life into account. Hennum (2014) maintains that one of the pitfalls social work with at-risk families entails is "...the instrumentalization of parents who are to fulfil their children's needs and raise them correctly, as defined by instruction given by professionals" (Hennum 2014, 452). Hennum also argues that the instructions given by professionals can lead to a "...hierarchy of knowledge privileging professional knowledge above parental ethno-theories and everyday life struggles" (Hennum 2014, 451).

Kousholt's (2011, 2012) study of family life shows that parents continuously arrange and rearrange routines according to changing and complex everyday life in order to make it work. Exploring such *action possibilities* (Dreier 2008) in everyday life together with the parents – including the parents' perspectives on everyday struggles – does not appear to be part of the professional interventions aimed at marginalised parents.

Concluding Discussion

From CPS' perspective, good parenthood includes regularity, stability and mothers fulfilling their children's needs in specific ways. This implies an understanding of children as a more or less passive individual dependent on the parents (mother). The point here is not to say that young children do not have needs, but that these needs are not universal, static or predictable independent of the concrete situation. On the contrary, children's needs are dynamic and situated in time and place. For parents, the intricacies of everyday life mean that they organise caring for their children in a complex collaboration that involves coordinating with multiple actors who contribute differently to the child care. The contributions of these actors also become a premise for family life and for the children's needs. Children's well-being is not just shaped by their parents but is co-created by various actors, such as day care workers, teachers, and other professionals. Conflicts and varying routines cannot be seen merely as a result of parents being disorganised or being unable to interpret and fulfil their children's needs. Instead, these conflicts are inevitably connected to the process of doing parenthood.

In order to navigate the contradictory and conflictual process of doing parenthood, parents can benefit from support in exploring children's varying needs and assistance with the challenges changing situations in family life offer. The instructions CPS gives to parents in the analysed case fail to sufficiently consider the degree of complexity and conflicting conditions that exist in everyday life. Instead the instructions offer a fixed, standardised understanding of good parenting and how to execute it. In Adam's case, CPS' approach appears to reinforce the challenges the family faces when trying to make everyday life work.

The analysis shows how good parenthood is defined by good motherhood (Nielsen and Westerling 2015), while fathers are largely excluded from the interventions. Moreover, it shows how interventions rely on a rather narrow, static understanding of parenthood, even though the field of family research has developed diverse understandings of parenthood as practical and processual in recent years (Marschall 2013; Morgan 1996; Finch 2007). When it comes to parenthood on the edge, diverse and manifold understandings of parenthood are regrettably absent.

NOTE

1. Translated from Danish by the author. Any references have been anonymised.

REFERENCES

Andenæs, A. 2011. "Chains of care: Organizing the everyday life of young children attending day-care." *Nordic Psychology* 63(2): 49–67.

Andenæs, A. 2012. "The task of taking care of children: Methodological perspectives and empirical implications." *Child & Family Social Work* 19(3): 263–271.

Corby, B., M. Millar, and L. Young. 1996. "Parental participation in child protection work: Rethinking the rhetoric." *British Journal of Social Work* 26(4): 475–492.

Daly, K., and A. Dienhart. 1998. "Family domain: Qualitative field dilemmas." In *Doing ethnographic research: Fieldwork settings*, edited by S. Grill, 97–120. Thousand Oaks: Sage.

Dreier, O. 2008. *Psychotherapy in everyday life: Learning in doing: Social, cognitive & computational perspectives.* Cambridge: Cambridge University Press.

Dumbrill, G. 2006. "Parental experience of child protection intervention: A qualitative study." *Child Abuse & Neglect* 30(1): 27–37.

Finch, J. 2007. "Displaying families." *Sociology* 41(1): 65–81.

Haavind, H. 2011. "Loving and caring for small children: Contested issues for everyday practices." *Nordic Psychology* 63: 24–48.

Hammersly, M., and P. Atkinsson. 2007. *Ethnography: Principles in practice.* 3rd edition. New York: Routledge.

Hennum, N. 2014. "Developing child-centered social policies: When professionalism takes over." *Social Sciences* 3: 441–459.

Højholt, C., and D. Kousholt. 2014. "Participant observations of children's communities: Exploring subjective aspects of social practice." *Qualitative Research in Psychology* 11(3): 316–334.

Holzkamp, K. 2013. "Psychology: Social self-understanding on the reasons for action in the conduct of everyday Life." In *Psychology from the standpoint of the subject: Selected writings of Klaus Holzkamp*, edited by E. Schraube and U. Osterkamp, 210–230. Basingstoke: Palgrave Macmillan.

Juhl, P. 2014. *På sporet af det gode børneliv.* [On the good life for children: Societal concerns and young children's perspectives on everyday life], Ph.D. thesis, Department of Psychology & Educational Studies. Roskilde: Roskilde University.

Kousholt, D. 2011. "Researching family through the everyday lives of children across home and day-care in Denmark." *Ethos (Malden)* 39(1): 98–114.

Kousholt, D. 2012. "Family problems: Exploring dilemmas and complexities of organising everyday family life." In *Children, childhood, and everyday life: Children's perspectives*, (edited by M. Hedegaard, K. Aronsson, C. Højholt, and O.S. Ulvik, 125–139. New York: Information Age Publishing.

Marschall, A. 2013. "Who cares for whom? Revisiting the concept of care in everyday life of post-divorce families." *Childhood* 21(4): 517–531.

Morgan, D.H.J. 1996. *Family connections.* Cambridge: Polity Press.

Nielsen, S.B., and A. Westerling. 2015. "Fathering as a learning process: Breaking new grounds in familiar territory." In *Fatherhood in the Nordic Welfare States: Comparing care policies and practice*, edited by G.B. Eydal and T. Rostgaard, 187–208. Bristol: Policy Press.

Singer, E. 1993. "Shared Care for Children." *Theory & Psychology* 3(4): 429–449.

Ulvik, O.S. 2007. *Seinmoderne fosterfamilier: En kulturpsykologisk studie av barn og voksnes fortellinger* [Late-modern foster families: A cultural-psychological study of childrens' and adults' naratives]. Oslo: Unipub forlag.

Woodhead, M. 1991. "Psychology and the cultural construction of 'Children's needs'." In *Growing up in a changing society*, edited by M. Woodhead, 37–53. London: Routledge.

Pernille Juhl, Ph.D., is Assistant Professor in the research programme Center for Childhood, Youth & Family Research at the Department of People & Technology, Roskilde University, Denmark. Her research interests are everyday family life; parenthood; children's everyday lives across contexts as families, at school and in day care; and social interventions focused on marginalised children and parents.

CHAPTER 5

Ambitious Parents as Ideal or Disorder: Doing Good Parenthood in Denmark and Singapore

Dil Bach

Abstract This chapter examines notions of good parenthood in Denmark and Singapore. As top scorers in the Programme for International Student Assessment (PISA) tests, the East Asian countries are a significant reference point in Scandinavian public debates about education and parenting. Education in East Asia is associated with highly ambitious parents and functions both as a source of inspiration and of concern in Denmark. Within the East Asian context, however, attitudes towards such highly ambitious parents are not unequivocally positive. In Singapore, for example, views of good parenthood are ambivalent and ideals are shifting somewhat towards the very norms often associated with Scandinavia, namely, a more relaxed approach focused on fostering children's social skills, creativity and well-being. This chapter explores how a shared perception of increasing global competition has led to opposing trends in educational reforms and changes in parenting norms in Denmark and Singapore respectively.

Keywords Singapore · Denmark · PISA · Civilising · Ambitious parenting · Kiasu parents

D. Bach (✉)
Department of Educational Anthropology, School of Education,
Aarhus University, Aarhus, Denmark
e-mail: dil@edu.au.dk

© The Author(s) 2016
A. Sparrman et al. (eds.), *Doing Good Parenthood*, Palgrave Macmillan
Studies in Family and Intimate Life, DOI 10.1007/978-3-319-46774-0_5

Based on ethnographic fieldwork in Denmark in 2005–2008 and in Singapore in 2013, this chapter explores changing notions of good parenthood.[1] In Scandinavia, globalisation is considered a challenge to established norms of education and parenting. Meanwhile, despite being top scorers in the PISA tests and therefore constituting "a significant other" (Mead [1934] 1992) in debates on education and parenting in, for example, Denmark, the East Asian countries have also begun to question their educational traditions and parenting norms. Unlike Denmark, however, the doubts in countries like Singapore are not about academic achievement. Rather, they focus on their system's inability to foster the creative, socially and emotionally competent individuals considered so necessary for future prosperity in the *global knowledge economy* (Bach and Christensen 2016). This chapter explores how the perceived demands of the *knowledge economy* have led to a common focus on education – especially early education – and on parents as good partners in education. However, the consequences in Denmark and Singapore have been seemingly contrasting educational strategies and changes in parenting norms.

The sociologist Annette Lareau introduces the concept *concerted cultivation* (2003, 2–3) to characterise the co-operation between middle-class families and schools in the USA. This concept is also relevant in relation to the parents from Denmark and Singapore who have participated in my research. Generally, they work together with schools and day cares on stimulating children academically, thus, transmitting cultural capital to them. This concept does not, however, capture the way home and school also work together – or are encouraged to do so – to help children become social and well-functioning. To capture this, I draw on sociologist Norbert Elias' concepts of *civilising* and *the civilised* (1998). *The civilised* refers to a society's dominant definition of good and proper, as opposed to wild and brutish, behaviour, while *civilising* concerns broader processes of transforming children into such proper human beings. In this way, *civilising* involves both cultivating and socialising processes, for instance, processes of building cultural, as well as social, capital and processes of integration and differentiation. Elias ([1939] 1994) suggests that a society's behavioural norms emanate from the upper strata which have led me to focus on middle- and upper-middle-class families.

The Study

This chapter is based on fieldwork in both Denmark and Singapore. In Denmark, my home country, I made contact with three upper-middle-class families on the periphery of my own social network. Via these families, I made contact with others in the same neighbourhood ending up with 15 families altogether. I interviewed 14 of the mothers, five of the fathers, seven children and two grandparents. Seven of the families, I interviewed just once, four of them twice, two of them five times and another two of them six times. All were interviewed in their homes, and I often participated in meals and other activities. Furthermore, I conducted more formalised participant observations with two of the families, visiting them ten times each and experiencing everything from morning to bedtime rituals. Finally, I interviewed four local child professionals and one au pair girl on their perceptions of good parenthood.

In Singapore, I arrived as a foreign scholar and made contact with parents through preschools, public meetings and colleagues at my host university. In total, I carried out interviews with 20 parents from Chinese, Indian and Malay backgrounds. In this chapter, I focus on middle-class Chinese families. In Singapore, I experienced a great interest in Nordic pedagogy and I gave several talks on the topic during my 3 months stay. Conversely, after returning home, I saw a programme on Danish national television in which a Danish and a Chinese school class competed. I became interested in the way East Asia is depicted in Danish educational policy and debate and searched newspapers, magazines and the Internet for chapters on the topic. This analysis is therefore, to a lesser degree, also based on public debates and policy documents. At the policy level, both in Denmark and Singapore, mothers and fathers are considered equally important as partners in education. I therefore use the term *parenting*, although in practice, parenting among my informants primarily involves mothers.

Contested Parenting Norms in Denmark

Denmark has a long tradition for a kindergarten pedagogy that focuses on play and the development of social skills, and a growing tradition of parental involvement whereby parents are expected to support this kindergarten pedagogy by participating in social events, making playdates or hosting birthday parties (Gilliam and Gulløv, Forthcoming). During my fieldwork, I found that parents also emphasised play and social skills in their parenting practices and in what they perceived to be the task of the kindergarten. When I asked a social educator[2] to describe what I would experience in the kindergarten during the afternoon, as parents began to pick up their children, the central role of play and social competences in parenting was evident.

> Hanne, social educator: You will experience some parents who are really good at letting their children finish playing... Parents who are engaged and interested in what the children have been doing... And who are friendly and inclusive.

However, the increased political perception of global competition and the apparent economic significance of early childhood education has led to kindergarten reforms in Denmark, and the question is often debated whether a *schoolification* of day care institutions is taking place (Kampmann 2005). In 2004, new learning curriculum was introduced in Danish day care institutions, by law, for the first time in history. And in 2012, a *Task Force on Future Day Care* (Task force for fremtidens dagtilbud 2012) submitted its recommendations on how to ensure better learning in day care and how to bring more learning into preschool children's lives. One of the central strategies for reaching these goals is to get parents to contribute. This was formulated by the former minister of education, "We must focus more on parents' active commitment to their children's learning... It might be to say that one should be reading for 20 minutes each day with one's child" (Krogh et al. 2012).

The Danish public school is also changing. A growing number of tests have been introduced in the last decade, and in 2009 school became compulsory from age 6 instead of age 7. In 2013, a new school reform was passed, which has resulted in a significantly longer school day. One objective is that children in eighth grade in the future should be able to master what children in the past used to in ninth grade (Aftale mellem regeringen 2013).

It is remarkable how the image of East Asia – often mediated by the PISA tests – comes into play in relation to these processes of change. "We can learn a lot from Singapore", said the minister of education after a summit of the world-leading nations in education (Antorini 2014). In another speech, she explicitly described how the government had also looked to the East when designing the recent school reform, "We have looked to the other Nordic countries and Canada. But those who are at the top are the Asian countries" (Trier 2013). However, the president of the association *School and Parent*, which represent parents' interests, articulates some differences between politicians' goals and those of parents, "For parents, it's not about getting their children to be clever enough to beat the Chinese in PISA tests. The holistic development of children is more important" (Jessen 2014). Similarly, a father commented on Facebook on the minister's proposal for daily reading with young children, "How about letting the kids be kids. We don't want things like in China with lots of child suicides" (Haugaard 2012). And in an article on the growing trend of private tutoring in Scandinavia, educational anthropologist Niels Kryger (2014) writes, "The question is whether we want a situation like in Singapore where parents compete in buying private tuition for their children, so that they can get ahead in the 'competition state'."

Thus, East Asia figures as both an inspiring Other and a source of concern in the Danish debate and is associated with highly ambitious parents. So far, high ambitions have not occupied a central position among parenting norms in Denmark. From both Danish parents' and educators' perspectives, good parenthood is performed by parents who spend time with their children, are not too strict and engage in their children's schools and day cares in a balanced manner (Bach 2015). This ideal is influenced by educational discourses in which homework, for example, is considered a family project. But good parenthood is first and foremost connected to an anti-authoritarian and psychologically inspired mind-set where playing with friends from school or kindergarten and lots of parental contact are considered prerequisites for a good childhood, and thus crucial for children's wholesome development, imagination and social competences. As parenting thus involves more than the building and transmission of cultural capital, I describe it as a *civilising process* (Bach 2015).

In this sense, parents in Denmark do not primarily act as unpaid teachers for their children, but rather as social educators. It is telling that Danish parents were reticent about expressing ambitions on their children's behalves or discussing their career prospects. This was somehow considered *uncivilised*. One father, Peter, emphasised that he did not care whether his children ended up as government ministers or labourers, just as long as they were happy. But then he added, in a whisper, "I'd prefer them to be ministers." Another parent, Anne, explicitly distanced herself from ambitious families, "I dislike children having to perform – in these superficial families. I really fear for what it does to the children." Danish parents were also reluctant to claim intellectual merit for their children. When I asked them how their children might make them proud, parents emphasised that their children were popular, creative and/or good at playing (Bach 2015). As Camilla said:

> Camilla: Christopher (8 years) is so good at playing... He is good at playing with things. He has all sorts of setups made of small wooden blocks. He is so creative... If he gets frustrated by the computer, I'll tell him not to use it for the next week, and he just starts playing with his toys. And he is really, really good at it. If he has friends over, they will play too. And when their parents come to pick them up, they'll be, like: "God, you haven't played on the computer at all," because their children are really, like, computer-children.

Not only did the parents engage in their children's social lives by making playdates, they also participated in numerous social events at their children's schools and day cares. These events are meant to create network among the families, but my research (Bach 2015) concludes that it also divides parents into more or less engaged parents. In short, my material shows that good parents, in the Danish context, are parents who are socially engaged, prioritise play and are not too ambitious. Similarly, the anthropologist Laura Gilliam stresses that in Danish schools, parents and children are discouraged from being too ambitious (Gilliam and Gulløv Forthcoming). Both Gilliam and I explain this *civilising ideal* by reference to the strong egalitarian ethos in Scandinavia (Bach 2015; Gilliam and Gulløv Forthcoming). This might also explain why it generates strong reactions that the minister of education looks eastward when designing new policies. She thereby evokes images of highly ambitious parents and hence norms of parenthood that are very different from what has constituted the dominant ideal of parenthood until now.

AMBIVALENCE IN SINGAPORE

Within East Asia, meanwhile, ambitious parents are not considered unequivocally doing good parenthood. In this region, there have been various initiatives to reform school and preschool since the late 1990s. Reformers criticise the widespread use of tests, examinations and private tuition. Such practices are now considered detrimental to a good childhood and hence to the development of creativity and social and emotional competences, which are seen as key competitive factors in the global knowledge economy. In 2003, shortly before learning curriculums was introduced by law in Danish kindergartens, the Singaporean Ministry of Education introduced a play-curriculum framework for preschools. This framework is informed by a psychological understanding of early childhood as a unique phase of life with special developmental and learning requirements. The main message is that learning in preschool should address these needs rather than imitating school. Thus, the idea of *learning through play* permeates the document (Bach and Christensen 2016).

In 2012, at roughly the same time as the Danish Task Force on Future Day Care recommended more learning in children's lives, the Singaporean Ministry of Education issued a revised version of the play-curriculum framework. While the thinking in the new document is similar to the thinking of 2003, there is significantly greater focus on parents. This may be linked to a heightened perception that children's lives have not become filled with joy, friends and playful learning in the intervening years (Bach and Christensen 2016). According to policymakers and educators, parents are the main culprits. "We need to change the mind-set of parents", they often told me. Singaporean educational reformers' view of parents is best summed up by the term *kiasu* parents. This refers to a local version of Amy Chua's concept of *the tiger mother* (2011). Kiasu parents are parents who want their children to get ahead at any price and who pressure them to achieve exam results that give access to prestigious schools and, later, well-paid jobs. Educators and policymakers portray *kiasu* parents as the primary obstacle to the success of the educational reform. Efforts to encourage parents to identify with a child-centred and psychologised parenting model have therefore become a key aspect of education policy. The ministry of education urges parents to communicate more intimately with their children and, instead of asking what they learned today, to ask them "what did you play?"

In this sense, the educational policy involves a new civilising ideal for both children and parents. As Singapore's Prime Minister cautioned parents in his 2012 national speech – around the same time as the Danish minister urged parents to read more with their young children:

> Please let your children have their childhoods!...Education experts, child development specialists, they warn against over teaching preschool children. You do harm, you turn the kid off, you make his life miserable...No homework is not a bad thing. It is good for young children to play and to learn through

> play. So please ... I read of parents who send their kindergarten age children to tuition, please do not do that (Lee in Bach and Christensen 2016).

Thus, Singaporean politicians increasingly characterise highly ambitious parents as uncivilised. And in a sense, the parents do the same. They struggle with *kiasuism*: some view it almost as a disorder from which they suffer. One mother, Sirene, prayed for God to help her become more relaxed. In this way, the psychological perspective on parenthood is already part of middle-class Chinese parents' own worldview. They typically describe the good parent as someone who is empathetic to their children, but this does not replace kiasuism. "We are all kiasu", parents often told me, but also that they were not "cool" about it.

Some parents, however, had almost stopped being *kiasu*. Joanna believed that constant pressure from her had given her eldest son a phobia of maths. She now considered herself relatively relaxed but felt that other parents discredited her. Her family would soon be going to the USA for 2 years and would return home just before the eldest son was to take a decisive exam (the PSLE[3]), "I talk with my friends, and some discourage me from going ... They think I'm selfish going to the States where we will be enjoying ... putting no more effort into their studies". Such comments affected Joanna. As other relatively relaxed parents, she doubted whether she was doing enough when other parents talked about all the private tuition they would be sending their children to. She was looking forward to escaping for a while from these competitive conversations with other Singaporeans.

More often, parents experienced the encounter with primary school as making them *kiasu*. "You want to be this way, but you might not be able to" said Alexis, mother of three children, and "I'll try not to stress my child too much, but if I don't stress her, she will tend to relax; she will tend to become playful" said Lucy, mother of two. Such comments were typical statements from the Singaporean parents that I interviewed. This testifies to the fact that many parents felt torn between two different ideals of good parenthood. According to the parents, the school took it for granted that children can read, write and count when they start in primary one. In this sense, many parents experienced a gap between the messages of joy and playful learning in preschool and the reality that confronted them in primary school. This was particularly true of Pam:

> Pam had experienced her eldest son's transition to primary school as a nightmare that shook up all her ideas about good parenthood. On the one

hand, she told me how the government idealised parents who gave their children a happy childhood, but on the other, that children of such parents suffered when they started in primary school. Until now, Pam had tried not to get caught up in the rat race by not sending her children for extra tuition, "I said 'No, my child is going to have a happy childhood.' And now he is in school, and he has [extra] Chinese class. I can't say, 'Well just continue to be happy', because he's going to fall behind."

This realisation had also made Pam change her practice in relation to her 3-year-old son, who had also begun to attend extra lessons in Chinese. Pam allowed him to remain in play-oriented childcare, but she pushed him at the same time.

> Pam: I still believe it shouldn't be like this... He learns Chinese in the day care, isn't that enough? But obviously my very short experience of primary school has told me that it's not enough, because there are all these other crazy parents who are pushing their children and the school expects you to know a lot by the time you get in, so if my child doesn't know, my child is going to suffer in primary one.

Like other parents, Pam explained that she herself had had a very strict mother. As a child, she had always wanted a different mother. Now she felt disorientated. She wished to be the mother she had wanted her own mother to be – a loving mother, not excessively focused on academic achievement. Since her eldest son had started school, however, she was beginning to become like her own mother. She wanted to be a good mother in her son's eyes, but in Singapore's education system, she felt this would mean letting him down. In her words, "If I didn't do that now, like pushing him and scolding him and being very fierce with him..., then I would have failed as a mother."

Pam had also begun to re-evaluate her view of her own mother. She now thought that it was thanks to her mother's pressure that she herself had had success career-wise. This gave rise to a different definition of the good mother, "she is a very good mother, because she sacrificed a lot of herself to push her children." What she had sacrificed was having a loving relationship with her children, and Pam now worried that this would be repeated. Like other Singaporean parents, Pam thus had ambivalent views on what signified good parenthood: she wanted to be the kind of parent proposed by the education reform, but at the same time, the government's own policy in schools forced her to be the *kiasu* parent that it increasingly portrays as uncivilised. In this way, the educations system's contradictory messages were pulling Pam and other Singaporeans apart between two conflicting ideals of good parenthood, namely the highly ambitious *kiasu* parent and the more relaxed, psychologically influenced parent.

Concluding Discussion

During these years, major changes are taking place in the field of education and parenting in both Scandinavia and East Asia. In Denmark, East Asian countries such as China and Singapore figure prominently in public policy and debate. The East Asian countries evoke images of highly ambitious parents and function as both an inspiring Other and a source of concern in Denmark, where explicit academic ambition has not previously been central to norms of good parenthood. In Singapore, however, the highly ambitious parent is not unequivocally considered good. On the contrary, good parenthood in Singapore is ambivalent and new civilising ideals have been introduced. Side by side with the *kiasu* parent exists a Scandinavian-inspired psychological model for more relaxed parenting. While an anti-authoritarian and psychology-based parenting ideal has hitherto been dominant in Denmark, this might now be under pressure. However, it is important to stress that good parenthood in Denmark has not meant completely relaxed parenting. Rather than competing academically, middle-class Danish parents compete on social engagement and on their children's social and creative competences.

In summary, this chapter has demonstrated how a shared perception of global competition has led to paradoxical mirroring processes, and how, from different starting points, it has resulted in apparently opposing trends in educational reforms and ideals of good parenthood in Denmark and Singapore. While politicians in Denmark prepare for the future by inculcating parents with academic ambitions, reformers in Singapore try to make the country future ready by urging parents to relax and give their children a happy childhood. However, neither in Denmark nor in Singapore are the politicians' attempts to predict what the future demands necessarily in accordance with the parents' own definitions of good parenthood.

Notes

1. The fieldwork in Singapore was supported by FOA under Grant [12/ 233071].
2. In Denmark, child professionals in kindergartens are social educators (pedagogues) rather than teachers.
3. The Primary School Leaving Examination.

References

Aftale mellem regeringen (Socialdemokratiet, Radikale Venstre og Socialistisk Folkeparti), Venstre og Dansk Folkeparti om et fagligt løft af folkeskolen. [Agreement on the academic improvement of the Danish elementary school]. Drafted June 7, 2013. http://www.kl.dk/ImageVault/Images/id_62271/scope_0/ImageVaultHandler.aspx: Accessed 21May 2016.

Antorini, C. 2014. "International videndeling om gode skoler er nyttigt" [International sharing of knowledge is useful]. Blog on *Folkeskolen.dk*. https://www.folkeskolen.dk/543281/international-videndeling-om-gode-skoler-er-nyttigt. Last modified 3 April 2014. Accessed 31 May 2016.

Bach, D. 2015. *Overskudsfamilier: Om opdragelse, identitet og klasse blandt velstående familier i Nordsjælland* [Alpha families. On parenting, identity and class among wealthy families north of Copenhagen]. Aarhus: Aarhus Universitetsforlag.

Bach, D., and S. Christensen. 2016. "Battling the Tiger Mother: Preschool reform and conflicting norms of parenthood in Singapore". *Children & Society*. doi:10.1111/chso.1216: 1-10.

Chua, A. 2011. *Kampråb fra en tigermor* [Battle hymn of the Tiger Mother]. Copenhagen: Gads forlag.

Elias, N. (1939) 1994. *The civilizing process.* Oxford: Blackwell.

Elias, N. 1998. "The civilizing of parents." In *The Norbert Elias reader*, edited by J. Goudsblom and S. Menell,189–211. Oxford: Blackwell.

Gilliam, L., and E. Gulløv. Forthcoming. *Children of the welfare state: Civilising practices in schools, childcare and families.* London: Pluto Press.

Haugaard, K. 2012. Entry on C. Antorini's facebook page. https://www.facebook.com/antorini/posts/386247678079289 [Post lated deleted by user]. Accessed May 25.

Jessen, B. 2014. "Lunkne forældre: Venter der en bedre skole efter sommerferien" [Luke-warm parents: Can we expect a better school after the summer break?] *Berlingske*, June 25. http://www.b.dk/nationalt/lunkne-foraeldre-venter-der-en-bedre-skole-efter-sommerferien.

Kampmann, J. 2005. "Understanding and theorizing modern childhood in Denmark: Tendencies and challenges". In *Frontrunners or Copycats?* edited by B. Tufte, J. Rasmussen, and L.B. Christensen, 20–37. Holbæk: Copenhagen Business School Press.

Krogh, K., S. Bendtsen, and U. Gunge, 2012. "Skrappere krav til småbørnsforældre" [Tougher demands on parents of toddlers]. *Berlingske*, May 21. http://www.b.dk/nationalt/skrappere-krav-til-smaaboernsforaeldre.

Kryger, N. 2014. Lektier skaber stress og ulighed. [Homework produces stress and inequality]. *Asterisk* 72: 32–33.

Lareau, A. 2003. *Unequal childhood: Class, race and family life*. Berkeley: University of California Press.

Mead, G.H. (1934) 1992. *Mind, self & society from the standpoint of a social behaviourist*. Chicago: University of Chicago Press.

Task force for fremtidens dagtilbud. 2012. *Fremtidens dagtilbud – Pejlemærker fra Task Force om Fremtidens Dagtilbud* [Future day care: Points of orientation from task force on future day care]. Copenhagen: Ministeriet for Børn og Undervisning.

Trier, M.B. 2013. Antorini: Reformen bør hæve danske Pisa-resultater. [Antorini: Reforms should raise Danish Pisa scores]. *Folkeskolen*, December 3. https://www.folkeskolen.dk/537423/antorini-reformen-boer-haeve-danske-pisa-resultater.

Dil Bach, Ph.D., is Assistant Professor at the Department of Educational Anthropology, School of Education, Aarhus University, Denmark, and is affiliated with the Danish Centre for Research into Early Childhood Education and Care, Roskilde University. Her research focuses on parenting and the relation between parents and (pre)schools in Denmark and Singapore. She has an interest in parenting, identity and class. Bach has recently contributed to the book *Children of the Welfare State: Civilizing Practices in Schools, Childcare and Families* (2016).

CHAPTER 6

Ambiguous Involvement: Children's Construction of Good Parenthood

Karen Ida Dannesboe

Abstract Increased focus on parents' responsibility for their children's education, and demands for more parental involvement in schools, have changed the role of parents in schools. This chapter explores the role of parents and norms of parenthood in relations between family and school. While the role of parents in their children's school is often studied from professionals' or parents' perspectives, this study focuses on constructions of good parenthood from children's perspectives. What do children expect of their parents' involvement with their school life? Based on ethnographic research in a Danish context, the study demonstrates that what defines a *good school parent* from children's perspectives involves support on demand and adult ambassadorship. It also shows that children's views of the good parent contradict teachers' versions of good parenthood, and that balancing diverse ideals of parenthood is a central aspect of contemporary parenthood.

Keywords Children's perspectives · School-family relations · Parental involvement · Ethnography

K.I. Dannesboe (✉)
Department of Educational Anthropology, School of Education,
Aarhus University, Aarhus, Denmark
e-mail: kida@edu.au.dk

© The Author(s) 2016
A. Sparrman et al. (eds.), *Doing Good Parenthood*, Palgrave Macmillan
Studies in Family and Intimate Life, DOI 10.1007/978-3-319-46774-0_6

Within the Danish welfare state, the institutionalisation of childhood and the organisation of children's lives in various institutions such as preschool and school have affected the relationship between state and families in three ways. First, professionals have taken over educational issues from parents (Rasmussen 2009). Second, the state has gained an increased interest in the family in various areas, including health and education. And third, the family has become an object of state intervention and public debate (Faircloth 2014; Kryger and Ravn 2009; Popkewitz 2001). Today, professionals and experts guide parents' actions and attitudes in childcare and educational matters (Faircloth 2014; Lee 2014). In Denmark as well as other Western countries, this tendency is reflected in increased demands for more parental involvement in school and blurred boundaries between school and family (Crozier 2005; Dannesboe 2013; Knudsen 2010). This development also has an impact on what is recognised as good parenthood by different actors, such as child professionals and parents themselves. The role of parents and norms of good parenthood in school are often discussed from a teachers' or parents' perspective, while children's experiences of their parent's involvement in school are less well explored. We know little of children's views on their parents' increased involvement in school and education. To cover this area, this chapter explores the following questions: How do children construct the role of their parents with regard to their school life? And what ideals of good parenthood are reflected in these constructions?

The Study

The chapter draws on empirical material from ethnographic fieldwork among Danish schoolchildren near Copenhagen conducted in 2006–2008. In a Danish context, parent-teacher cooperation is organised around individual children and the activities taking place in children's school classes. Therefore, the ethnographic study was conducted within a school class with approximately 26 children aged 12–14.[1] The fieldwork includes observations of everyday life in school, parent-teacher activities and visits in 11 families as well as interviews with children, parents and teachers. Besides informal conversations with children, parents and teachers, 52 interviews were conducted with three teachers, 14 parents and 24 children – with most of the children being interviewed two to three times. The empirical data consists of field notes, transcriptions of interviews and transcriptions of parent-teacher conferences as well as photographs taken by the children of their school life. The methodological issues and ethical concerns regarding ethnographic fieldwork and research methods have been discussed elsewhere (see Dannesboe 2012). For this chapter, I have revisited my empirical data and focused more closely on children's constructions of their parents' role in their school lives. The analysis is mainly based on observations from parent-teacher conferences and from family visits as well as interviews and informal conversations with the children, while the rest of the empirical material serves as a background in the analytical process. In the analysis, examples represent dominant tendencies in the data.

ANALYTICAL FRAMEWORK: FAMILY STUDIES AND CHILDHOOD RESEARCH

The analytical framework is inspired by new anthropological and socio-logical studies of families and childhood research. Family studies empha-sise that the family is a construction made through social practices and relationships (Carsten 2000; Finch 2007; Morgan 1996). In a similar manner, Parenting Culture Studies stress parenting practices in a social, cultural and historical context (Lee et al. 2014). While these approaches provide inspiration for analysing good parenthood as a lived practice performed by family members and child professionals, they often neglect children's participation and contributions. To address the way in which children act as co-producers of parenthood, this study also draws on anthropological and sociological childhood research. This means a strong focus on children's personal experiences and comprehensions of everyday lives, as well as a focus on how central conditions influence children's actions and opportunities (e.g. James and Prout 1997). School-family relations and parental involvement are some of the important conditions influencing contemporary childhood and children's everyday lives. Exploring good parenthood in school-family relations from children's perspectives emphasises children's experiences and thoughts about parents' involvement with school.

Studies drawing on childhood and family research emphasise children's participation in and contribution to complex family relations (James and Curtis 2010; Mason and Tipper 2008; Winther et al. 2014). For instance, a study of family displays (cf. Finch 2007) stresses that family practices can be described in different ways by children and adults and are embedded in notions of doing family properly (James and Curtis 2010). Likewise, I will argue that family-school relations and parents' roles in school can be described and experienced differently by children and adults. As I will show in this chapter, children and teachers have different ideas of what counts as a good parent.

PARENTS AS AMBASSADORS

Doing fieldwork among children, I was struck by an apparent ambiguity in their expressions about their parents' involvement in school. On the one hand, parents could be embarrassing at parent-teacher conferences, and they could be annoying when they interfered too much in school life. On the other hand, almost all the children in the study also valued their parents' involvement in their school life. This led me to explore what children can teach us about good parenthood more generally and good school parenting specifically.

When it comes to parental involvement in children's school life, what seems to matter is not so much the quantity of involvement but the character of this involvement. Parents do receive some information about school from their children. But they also receive information about their children's academic performance and social well-being no matter how often (or how much) children talk with their parents. There is a constant flow of information from teachers to parents in bi-annual parent-teacher conferences, newsletters or daily news and messages on the Parents' Intranet (a digital communication platform used by most state schools in Denmark, see Akselvoll this volume). A handful of children in the study described how information provided by teachers sometimes resulted in quarrels with their parents about their behaviour in school or participation in lessons. Despite such experiences, almost all the children explain that they want their parents to know about their school situation and about the ways in which the teachers evaluate their performance. As one boy, Oliver, explains: "Your parents get to know you better when they are informed about good and bad aspects of school life by the teachers". Another child, Julie, explains why this knowledge is important:

> I tell my mother what she ought to know [...]. Because I think your parents, well they don't know what their child is like in school if they don't know anything about the school environment

From Julie's and Oliver's points of view, information about school life provides their parents with important and specific knowledge about them as school children. Information about school is a way to know them even better. So why is parental knowledge about them as school children so important? One of the boys, Nicolai, gives an answer to this: "It makes me feel safe when my parents know about school stuff". Across the interviews and observations, it is clear that the feeling of being safe is connected to their experiences of having someone to turn to in school matters. For instance, a majority of the children in the class describe how they appreciate their parents helping them with difficult school issues, for instance conflicts with friends, classmates or teachers. According to these children, parents are able to help because, as they say: "my parents know what I'm like." Being a good parent in such cases seems to involve being a parent with knowledge of the child as a family child and as a school child. The good parent also knows how to combine this knowledge to improve the child's school situation.

Parents' knowledge about their child is important not only in daily interactions with their children but also in meetings with teachers. The ethnographic observations and interviews illustrate that parents' communication with teachers can help to strengthen children's own voices. In particular, a handful of children in the class emphasise the importance parents have when speaking on their behalf in discussions with the teachers. They argue that parent' statements have much greater impact on the teachers than children's own statements. As expressed by Oliver: "Things are taken more seriously if adults [parents] say them than if a child tells you something." The fact that children regard this as being a proper parent can also be illustrated through the case of Natasja and her mother. During a parent-teacher conference, Natasja's mother brings up a controversy about Natasja's attitude towards the teacher in the maths class. The teacher describes Natasja's approach as problematic and conflictual. Before starting the meeting with the teacher, Natasja and her mother have discussed the controversy at home. At the meeting, where Natasja is present, her mother explains how Natasja feels about the situation and why Natasja acts the way she does. Afterwards Natasja describes the meeting:

> My mum takes me seriously no matter what. It's nice to know that you have someone to talk to and are listened to. And it's nice that she does something about it instead of just telling me, "well it will change in time".

As this quotation illustrates, the mother does not just listen, she also acts upon the child's descriptions of what is going on in school. In this sense, a good parent is constructed as a trustworthy spokesperson with the important qualification of being an adult – an adult to whom the teacher has to listen. Cases like these show how parents act as ambassadors for their children in school-family meetings. Furthermore, the case of Natasja illustrates another important aspect of being a good parent. When Natasja's mother confronts the teacher, she is being loyal to Natasja's point of view on the controversy. She uses her capacity to speak up in solidarity with her daughter instead of agreeing with the teacher's perspective on the situation. In this way, a good parent can also be described as the child's ally in the sense that they help children to confront teachers with issues of importance and show solidarity with their children. Following this argument, a good parent should be the children's ally instead of being an ally of the school.

Finch defines family display as "the process by which individuals, and groups of individuals, convey to each other and to relevant audiences that certain of their actions constitute 'doing family things' and thereby confirm that these relationships are 'family' relationships" (Finch 2007, 67). In the case of Natasja and her mother, it is not family relationships that are displayed and confirmed in front of the teacher but a kind of parent-child solidarity. A solidarity that is not necessarily recognised by the teachers as proper parenthood but is a central aspect of good parenthood in children's perspectives. Just as family displays are embedded in a broader cultural context with certain notions of good parenthood (James and Curtis 2010), children's constructions of what counts as a good parent in relation to the school are also embedded in the school as a social, cultural and institutional context. In this context, other constructions of good parenthood take place. In a school context, the expectations of teachers regarding the role of parents in school also reflect ideals of parenthood. One dominant ideal among school teachers defines good parents as people who assist the school by supporting their own child's academic progress as well as the social community of the class (Dannesboe 2012). Parents who focus too much on their own child and ask too many questions are defined as demanding and lacking the necessary insights into the social community of the whole school class (Knudsen 2010). Being a good parent from the teacher's point of view means acting as a school ally. This attitude reflects the idea that parents should be the school's ambassadors rather than their children's ambassadors. Thus, the analysis shows a tension between the perspectives of children and teachers with regard to parents' attention and loyalties.

The existence of ambiguous demands about loyalty illustrates the fact that different ideals of parenthood co-exist and that parents' practices can be interpreted differently according to such ideals.

SOCIAL EVENTS AND SUPPORT ON DEMAND

Both teachers and parents often regard homework as a central aspect of parental involvement. As already mentioned above, teachers want parents to be good school ambassadors. Teachers expect parents to keep up with the flow of information, for instance, regarding homework. They also expect parents to use this information to assist children's academic progress (Dannesboe 2012). Homework is more or less regarded as part of parents' parental duty and is thereby part of doing parenthood (Bach 2015; Forsberg 2007; McCarthy and Kirkpatrick 2005; Solomon et al. 2002). The children in this study are also concerned with the influence parents have on homework practices. On the one hand, children do not want to be monitored by their parents. They do not want them to interfere with homework. On the other hand, they also express appreciation when parents help out with homework when needed. Below, I elaborate on ideals of parenthood that are revealed in these two somewhat conflicting ways of relating to homework.

According to five of the children, homework is described as a social event that combines getting help with sharing family-parent-child time. One girl, Signe, explains how she does homework with her little brother and her father all sitting around the dining table. She describes the situation as "cosy". Her father is not just a homework assistant with skills relevant for school but also creates a cosy atmosphere. He is accessible and is involved with the children's school assignments. In this case, the good parent is constructed as being helpful, present and caring. Furthermore, the case indicates how ideals of being a good school parent bring together and intertwine family life, shared social experiences and homework (see also Solomon et al. 2002).

However, a majority of the children have a different view on parents and homework. They will do anything to limit parental involvement. They do homework on their own, often in their own room, and only bring up homework issues with their parents when absolutely necessary. These children describe parents who interfere in homework issues without being invited as annoying: parental help is only welcome when children ask for it. Johan explains that he avoids bringing up homework as a topic at home, as he fears his mother's interference will limit his options and freedom to choose where and when he can do it. Children's negotiation of where and when homework should be done is also a negotiation about independence and managing school on their own. In such cases, parents' roles are reduced to providing support on demand. This suggests that being a good parent from a children's perspective means being available and allowing space for independence instead of pursuing an agenda belonging to parents or teachers.

LIMITED PARENTAL INVOLVEMENT

Many of the children want to limit their parents' involvement not only in their homework but also in other school matters. A frequent and often repeated theme in the interviews is avoiding parents who cause feelings of insecurity or who create unpleasant situations. This is specifically emphasised in relation to the lack of control of the information flow between parents and teachers. Many of the children describe how it makes them feel embarrassed at parent-teacher conferences when their teachers or parents reveal aspects of children's lives to each other without warning. In the words of Johan, it can make them feel "busted". To avoid such situations, most children have strategies to control the information flow between teachers and parents. For instance, they deliberately forget to deliver messages or report episodes that could be embarrassing or cause trouble. Their strategies reflect children's concern with and wish to control their parents' knowledge about school and school life (Alldred et al. 2002; Dannesboe 2012). Children's strategies to control information and avoid what they experience as an unpleasant situation illustrate that a good parent has relevant information about school life but that this information should not be unknown to the child. A good parent does not ask the teacher too many questions, nor does she or he reveal too much about their child's lives without the permission of the child. She or he respects children's limits with regard to what they wish to share and when they wish to share information about their school life.

CONCLUDING DISCUSSION

In a Danish context, parents have never been more involved in their children's school than today. Parental involvement is a condition of being a parent. As illustrated in this chapter, the desired extent and intensity of parental involvement reflects diverse ideals of parenthood. By exploring children's descriptions and experiences of their parents' role in school-family relations, this study has shown that from a children's perspective good parenthood is characterised by showing solidarity with children and being supportive when needed by children, thus respecting children's independence. I have argued that a good parent acts as an ambassador and a children's ally. In these terms, a good school parent is a parent who is attentive and available, but with a limited involvement; a parent who knows when and how to act based on children's needs. In other words, a good school parent is an attentive adult who is involved in school on children's terms.

The chapter also illustrates the complexity and ambiguity of good parenthood. The analysis illustrate, that good parenthood is being done in multiple ways by different actors. What is defined as good is both situational and dependent on the perspective from which parenthood is understood. Children's perspectives on good parenthood seem to challenge the school's ideals of good parenthood. First of all, the children's view that a good parent is a parent with a limited involvement challenges the dominant ideal of a good parent as someone who is greatly involved in school life and always ready to support school issues in family life. Second, the children's view that a good parent is a child ambassador and children's ally in school challenges dominant discourses of school-family relations in which parents are expected to support the school and act as the school's ambassador in the family. From a school perspective, a good parent is someone who acts on behalf of the school. Whereas teachers often emphasise parental involvement as a way to support the school, children are more likely to see parental involvement as a way to display solidarity with children. In this sense, different and even conflicting ideals of parenthood co-exist. To act as a parent according to different parenthood ideals can be challenging. To be loyal to your child might be understood by the teachers as inappropriate and as a lack of support of the school.

In a broader sense, this study brings forward central aspects of contemporary parenthood. For instance, it stresses the complexity of parents' role in contemporary society and the difficult task of balancing between different ideals of good parenthood. Furthermore, the study reveals how good parenthood is constructed within and beyond families and is deeply entangled with the institutions of the welfare state. Finally, the focus on children draws attention to the fact that good parenthood is not done by adults alone but is also influenced by children and their thoughts and actions.

NOTE

1. When I first met the children they were 12 years old, but when the fieldwork ended almost two years later most of them had turned 14.

REFERENCES

Alldred, P., M. David, and R. Edwards. 2002. "Minding the gap: Children and young people negotiating relations between home and school." In *Children, home and school: Regulation, autonomy or connection?* edited by R. Edwards, 121–137. London: Routledge/Falmer.

Bach, D. 2015. *Overskudsfamilier. Om opdragelse, identitet og klasse blandt velstående familier i Nordsjælland* [Alpha families. On parenting, identity and class among wealthy families north of Copenhagen]. Aarhus: Aarhus Universitetsforlag.

Carsten, J., ed. 2000. *Cultures of relatedness: New approaches to the study of kinship.* Cambridge: Cambridge University Press.

Crozier, G. 2005. "Beyond the call on duty: The impact of racism on black parents' involvement in their childrens's education." In *Activating participation: Parents and teachers working towards partnership*, edited by G. Crozier and D. Reay, 39–55. Stoke on Trent: Trentham books.

Dannesboe, K.I. 2012. *Passende engagement og (u)bekvemme skoleliv. Et studie af børns navigationer mellem skole og familie.* [Appropriate engagement and (dis)content school life. A study of children's navigation between school and family.] Ph.D. thesis, Department of Aarhus University.

Dannesboe, K.I. 2013. "Den grænseløse skole?" [The limitless school?] *Barn* 4: 45–60.

Faircloth, C. 2014. "Intensive parenting and the expansion of parenting." In *Parenting culture studies*, edited by E. Lee, J. Bristow, C. Faircloth, and J. Macvarish, 25–50. Basingstoke: Palgrave Macmillan.

Finch, J. 2007. "Displaying families." *Sociology* 41(1): 65–81.

Forsberg, L. 2007. "Homework as serious family business: Power and subjectivity in negotiations about school assignments in Swedish families." *British Journal of Sociology of Education* 28(2): 209–222.

James, A., and A. Prout. 1997. *Constructing and Reconstructing Childhood.* London: RoutledgeFalmer.

James, A., and P. Curtis. 2010. "Family displays and personal lives." *Sociology* 44(6): 1163–1180.

Knudsen, H. 2010. *Har vi en aftale? Magt og ansvar i mødet mellem folkeskole og familie* [Do we have an agreement? Power and responsibility in the meeting between Danish public schools and families]. Frederiksberg: Nyt fra Samfundsvidenskaberne.

Kryger, N., and B. Ravn. 2009. "Reinstalling state-governed adult authority?" *Nordisk Pædagogik*, 29(1): 163–173.

Lee, E. 2014. "Experts and parenting culture." In *Parenting culture studies*, edited by E. Lee, J. Bristow, C. Faircloth, and J. Macvarish, 51–75. Basingstoke: Palgrave Macmillan.

Lee, E., J. Bristow, C. Faircloth, and J. Macvarish, eds. 2014. *Parenting culture studies*. Basingstoke: Palgrave Macmillan.

Mason, J., and B. Tipper. 2008. "Being related: How children define and create kinship." *Childhood* 15(4): 441–460.

McCarthy, J.R., and S. Kirkpatrick. 2005. "Negotiating public and private: Maternal mediations of home-school boundaries." In *Activating participation: Parents and teachers working towards partnership*, edited by G. Crozier and D. Reay, 59–82. Stoke on Trent: Trentham Books.

Morgan, D. 1996. *Family connections*. Cambridge: Polity Press.

Popkewitz, T.S. 2001. "Pacts/partnerships and governing the parent and child." *Current Issues in Comparative Education* 3(2): 1–9.

Rasmussen, K.2009. "Om barndommens institutionalisering – og noget om dens affortryllelse." [On the institutionlization of childhood – and somtehing about it's disenchantment]. In *Barndommens organisering: I et dansk institutionsperspektiv* [The organization of childhood. A Danish perspective on institutions], edited by S. Højlund. Page, Frederiksberg: Roskilde Universitetsforlag.

Solomon, Y., J. Warin, and C. Lewis. 2002. "Helping with homework? Homework as a site of tension for parents and teenagers." *British Educational Research Journal* 28(4): 603–622.

Winther, I. W., C. Palludan, E. Gulløv, and M.M. Rehder. 2014. *Hvad er søskende? Praktiske og følsomme forbindelser* [What are siblings? Practical and sensitive relations]. København: Akademisk forlag.

Karen Ida Dannesboe, Ph.D., is Assistant Professor at the Department of Educational Anthropology, School of Education, Aarhus University, Denmark. Central research areas include childhood; relations between children, family and the Welfare State; materiality and identity. More specific research interests are children's everyday lives across institutions, the institutionalisation of childhood, school–family relations and parenthood.

CHAPTER 7

Limited But Committed Parents: Primary School Teachers Negotiating Good Parenthood in a Disadvantaged Area

Disa Bergnehr

Abstract This chapter scrutinises primary school teachers' discourse on good and poor parenthood in a disadvantaged area with a high percentage of migrant families. The analysis shows that teachers' notions of good parenthood are intertwined with their notions of parental involvement. In contrast with much of the existing literature, the analysis illustrates how the teachers repeatedly justify and excuse inadequate parental involvement. Moreover, they repeatedly reflect on how they, as teachers, can adapt their activities to suit the needs and wishes of parents. The study proposes that activities and informative measures, which facilitate parents' influence, contribute to parental involvement. Since parents are a heterogeneous group, school leadership and teachers have to take a flexible stance regarding involvement and good parenting. The results indicate that it is important to further investigate reciprocity in home–school relations and parental involvement.

Keywords Parental involvement · Home-school relations · Teacher discourse · Migrant families · Disadvantaged areas

D. Bergnehr (✉)
School of Health and Welfare, Jönköping University, Jönköping, Sweden
e-mail: Disa.Bergnehr@ju.se

© The Author(s) 2016
A. Sparrman et al. (eds.), *Doing Good Parenthood*, Palgrave Macmillan
Studies in Family and Intimate Life, DOI 10.1007/978-3-319-46774-0_7

From an early age, children in Sweden spend a considerable amount of time in state-regulated institutions such as preschools and schools (Wells and Bergnehr 2014). As noted by others (Bridges 2008; Coffey 2001), the education system is depicted in the political and public discourses as having the means to narrow societal gaps and promote public health by providing equal education and care (Bergnehr 2015a; Bergnehr and Nelson 2015). However, the gap has widened not only between children from high and low socioeconomic status (SES) homes but also between schools situated in different socioeconomic areas (Skolverket 2009; Statistics Sweden 2007). Home–school collaboration and parental obligations have been proposed as ways of reversing such negative trends, and they are increasingly accentuated in the Western world (Baez and Talburt 2008; Crozier 1998; Van Den Berg and Van Reekum 2011). This begs the following questions: What do contemporary schools expect from parents? How is good parenthood and poor parenthood done in home-school relations?

Previous research proposes that good parenthood is defined by doing the following: the parent or parents choose a school that provides an auspicious learning environment, they commit to rules that are determined by the school, they see to it that their child attends school, they supervise homework and encourage the child to study and behave according to the rules and values of the school (Crozier 1998). Additionally, parents prepare their child for the school day with regard to sleep, food, clothing, schoolbooks, sports equipment and so on (Lareau 2000). However, the parental conduct required for high achievement levels – that is middle-class parenting requiring specific social and economic resources – is, for some parents, just not possible (Lareau 2011). Increased expectations of parental involvement in children's schooling have had unfavourable implications for children from low SES homes and minority groups (Bergnehr 2012; Reay 2004). Teachers and school leaders are inclined to depict low SES parents as failing in their responsibilities towards schools or as difficult to cooperate with (Bouakaz 2008; Dahlstedt and Hertzberg 2011; Woods and Hammersley 1993).

The notion of the good parent appears to be connected to the child's level of achievement; parents of poorly achieving pupils run a high risk of being referred to as lacking in parental involvement (Van Den Berg and Van Reekum 2011). However, there are studies that paint a different picture. López et al. (2001) investigated four schools with high percentages of pupils of foreign origin. They concluded that the schools had not "subscribed to a particular definition of involvement", and that "they held themselves accountable to meet the multiple needs of migrant parents on a daily and on-going basis" (253). This is an example of schools that do not judge parental conduct as unsatisfactory based on a static definition of involvement and good parenthood. Rather, these schools offered support based on each family's specific needs, and school personnel formulated their expectations of parents in relation to the family's situation. This is quite the opposite of other findings of how schools generally define good parenthood: that parents are controlled by schools rather than partners on equal terms (for example, Crozier 1998; Crozier and Davies 2007; Edwards 2002).

THE STUDY

The present study investigates primary school teachers' discourse on good and poor parenthood.[1] The material was collected in a Swedish school located in a low SES area. More than 90 per cent of the pupils are of foreign origin and, consequently, the mother tongue of the majority of children and their parents is not Swedish. The pupils' levels of achievement are below the national average. In Sweden, overall, children who attend schools situated in low SES areas have a high risk of failing at school (Statistics Sweden 2007).

The data consist of almost 90 pages of field notes from observing 24 hours of naturally occurring conversations with a total of nine teachers. The teachers were participating in further education teacher training aimed at promoting propitious relationships between teachers and children and reducing bad behaviour in the classroom. The teachers' conversations about parents have been analysed. In addition, the data consist of two group interviews with seven teachers who did not attend the observed meetings but had attended similar further education teacher training. The guiding questions in the semi-structured interviews focused on home-school relations, the course content and the teachers' work. The interviews lasted about 60 minutes; they were tape-recorded and transcribed verbatim prior to their analysis. When presented in the results section, quotes from the notes/observations are labelled using letters, for example, Teacher A (Notes, meeting 1), while accounts from the interviews are labelled using numbers, for example, Teacher 1 (Interview 1).

The notes and interview transcripts have been analysed as discursive constructions that provide information on the teachers' understandings and negotiations of home-school relations, parental responsibilities and the schools' obligations. The discursive resources that the teachers apply are regarded as products of social and organisational contexts. They are seen as uniquely produced by the specific individuals at their particular schools and formed by these individuals' experiences as well as the particular situations in which the data were collected. The analysis of language is based on the notion that talking, both in speech and text, is a social action and "language is constitutive: it is the site where meanings are created and changed" (Taylor 2001, 6). The study of meaning-making processes through the study of discourse acknowledges the influence of context – meanings are negotiated, produced and reconstructed by certain individuals who are situated in certain contexts (Taylor 2001).

The analysis was started by coding the notes and interviews into instances containing talk about parents; such instances are more frequent in the interviews. The interview questions include the topics of home-school relations. The further education teacher training, where the notes are taken, centred on the teacher-pupil relationship and classroom activities. The scrutiny of instances regarding parents and home-school relations prompt discursive formulations on contextual matters, for example, school leadership, national inspections and goals, the work environment, the teachers' obligations and work aspirations, and parental conduct and involvement. Although all codes are taken into account, the analytical focus is on parental conduct and involvement. This provides a picture of the different and varying ways in which good and poor parenthood and teachers' and parents' responsibilities are articulated. The research questions are: In what ways are good and poor parenthood understood and negotiated? How do the teachers define their own and the parents' responsibilities and capabilities?

LIMITED BUT COMMITTED PARENTING

The positioning of parents as passive appears repeatedly in the data in varying ways; passivity is referred to as problematic. However, parental passivity is only connected to indifference towards their child's behaviour or school achievement in one instance. One teacher expressed frustration regarding a parent who, at a teacher-parent conference, did not openly agree with the teacher that their child being repeatedly late for school was a problem

(Teacher B, Notes, meeting 7). A more recurrent way of talking about parents was the expression of parents having resigned from their fostering responsibility. For instance, one teacher referred, with frustration, to the parents of a pupil who refused to participate in some compulsory activities.

> Teacher E: I have called the parents, I have used the interpreter but the parents say, "That is your responsibility as a teacher. She doesn't listen, so I don't know what to do," the father says, and the mother says, "Do what you want, what you think is best." OK, I'm in charge of this pupil two hours a week – am I going to raise her in this time? Because that's what the father said, more or less, raise her at school, during school hours. (Notes, meeting 2)

In the quote above, parental inadequacies are not explained or excused. However, when parents are referred to as passive in their commitment towards their child's schooling, it is usually combined with justifications such as the parents' lack of knowledge or their being hindered by limited resources. Thus, inadequate parental involvement is repeatedly justified, as in the following reasoning, where the teachers started out by discussing low attendance at general parent meetings.

Teacher I: I don't believe it's due to a lack of interest, most parents prioritise their children.
Teacher B: They may be tired.
Teacher H: And they have a lot of children, and perhaps they work evenings, they don't have the energy and it's difficult because who's going to mind the children at home? (Notes, meeting 1)

The teachers talk about the parents as being unable, not unwilling, to accomplish what is expected of them. For some, being involved in school, for example, by attending parent meetings, helping with homework or ensuring that their child gets to school on time, is problematic for many reasons. These reasons may include hours of work, a poor command of the Swedish language, restricted mobility, lack of energy because of single parenting and/or having many dependent children. Such wording is used in the interviews and discussions to justify parents' failure to commit to their child's schooling. This, however, does not preclude arguments that point out parents' conduct as being unsatisfactory. The following is an example.

Teacher 1: They may not always understand the obvious – that I, as a parent, have to support my child, that I must try to help with my child's homework. Like, the school is responsible for the child's learning, but, and this is where it becomes tricky, we communicate repeatedly the importance of parents being part of this and how they should support their child. Although you can't read yourself, you can let your child read out loud to you because reading skills require repetition. The school can't accomplish everything – the child must repeat continuously. This is where it becomes a bit difficult, it becomes a bit hard to handle and it's a slow process, because people come, perhaps from a totally different context where school was not that important, and suddenly the demands on them are quite large, because here school asks parents to be involved and committed. (Interview 1)

The quote above is a pertinent example of the dynamic positioning of parents. In this particular instance, parents' ignorance is initially referred to as being the problem since they do not support their child (or the school) despite the teacher's efforts. This stance is followed, and supported, by the phrase, "The school can't accomplish everything". The teacher continues by referring to circumstances that are difficult to influence, bridging with "This is where it becomes a bit difficult…" The argument changes from individualising the problem of parents who fail in their commitment to referring to structural factors such as lack of knowledge due to migration and the unfamiliar national context and educational system.

There are recurring instances where the teachers bring up increased support to parents as desirable. They argue that many parents need and want more information on what parenting and school attendance entail in Sweden. Consequently, the argument continues, parents need societal support to gain the required resources to become involved in their child's schooling in, for the school and teachers, desirable ways.

Teacher 5: For us it's easy, we make the rules here at school, how things should work, how the children should behave and act, but then they go home and it's black or white, the exact opposite. The parents don't know what to ask of their children, they don't know what we ask of their children. Their children fool them saying "It's ok to be out late", and skip the homework, or "I'll do my homework at my mates", or "I did the homework at school". They [the parents] don't really know how things work, it would be great to be able to tell them about such matters, so that the parents can say, "This is what you do at school, these are the rules at school, this is your homework, which must be done". (Interview 2)

Parental involvement and good parenthood are connected to parental authority and knowledge of the Swedish schooling system and society. In the best of worlds, the teachers argue, the school would be able to provide information that would support parents and be propitious for the parent-child relationship and home-school collaboration.

In the past few years, the school where the teachers work has received extra resources in terms of interpreters, so-called mediating teachers who are fluent in both Swedish and one of the major languages spoken by the families, for example Arabic. The teachers argue that these mediating teachers have been a great support to the children, parents and teachers alike in that their work has facilitated parental involvement. One example is as follows.

Teacher 4:   We could do with more mediating teachers. Because they are a great help.

Teacher 6:   Yes, particularly when cultural issues are discussed, for example, how you support your child's homework and all that parents have many, many questions about. Like, "Why is there so little homework?" They [the mediating teachers] are really important as they discuss the Swedish school system.

Teacher 4:   They have great, close contact with the parents. When you see them interact, you can tell the parents trust them and really listen to what they say. (Interview 2)

According to the teachers, home-school communication and parental involvement have been improved by the possibility of offering interpreted meetings and discussion groups in the parents' mother tongue, and by communicating with parents with the help of the mediating teachers.

The teachers continuously refer to the parents as being limited in a number of ways and say that, because of this, parents become somewhat passive or uninvolved. Nevertheless, at the same time, the teachers associate parents with positive attributes such as being open, engaged and committed. When the teachers discuss parents' attendance at parent meetings, they reflect on why attendance is sometimes high and at other times low, and why it is difficult to get a dialogue going with the parents.

Teacher A: It's really hard to get a conversation, an exchange of views, going. I spoke to an interpreter, and I said that no one [of the parents] says anything in meetings about their child's lack of achievement. They don't argue with teachers, so it's really hard.

> *Teacher B:*   And they are really grateful, "You're so great, so great". But then you get a bit like "I'm not that great". No Swedish parents would say that.
>
> *Teacher A:*   A dialogue is giving and taking, it's not like in other schools, where parents question just for the sake of it. It is difficult, but we have to create other kinds of meetings where we can communicate. (Notes, meeting 8)

Discussions about parent meetings and home-school conferences entailed reasoning as to how the teachers could better attract parents to meetings and promote dialogue with them by adjusting the content and/or the time of meetings. Thus, rather than positioning parental involvement as lacking because of parents' low attendance and/or involvement at meetings, the discussions involved reasoning as to how the teachers could adapt the events to better fit the needs and wishes of the parents. In one interview, the large number of parents present at the school's annual BBQ evening was brought up as a contrast to other general meetings. The parents were referred to in the following way.

> Teacher 7: They are fantastic, they are so incredibly generous. Like they want to offer us things in return. They don't want to sit down to get information, they bring their cookies, pastries from their home countries, and that makes them feel good, to offer us something in return, to bring something rather than to just sit down and listen. I'm not an expert on these things but that's how I interpret their behaviour – they want to give something back. (Interview 2)

The reasoning quoted above points out the relevance of conceptualising home-school relations as formed by reciprocity. That is, home-school relations must not be regarded as one-way communication. It appears imperative that there should be activities and situations that enable all involved parties to give and take, and that home-school relations should be based on the notion that both parents and teachers have resources and skills, inadequacies and needs. Reciprocity needs to be considered in future research.

CONCLUDING DISCUSSION

The present study provides a complex and nuanced picture of what schools expect of parents, and how teachers define good parenthood. The teachers refer to parental conduct both as lacking and poor and good and committed. In addition, they justify the parents' lack of involvement with the limits they face because of socioeconomic factors and their migrant status. This is in accordance with López, Scribner and Mahitivanichcha's (2001) work, which illustrates how school personnel strive to support disadvantaged, migrant families. There are studies on parental involvement and home-school relations which suggest that schools and teachers control and discipline parents (Crozier 1998; Edwards 2002), and/or that parental obligations towards schools have increased (Baez and Talburt 2008). However, the author and others have previously argued that the conduct of teachers is as controlled as that of parents, and is perhaps becoming increasingly so (Bergnehr 2012, 2015b). Nowadays, a teacher's competence is rated based on pupils' results in national tests, and schools are given the responsibility of counteracting social stratification and marginalisation by providing care and education for all (Bridges 2008; Coffey 2001). The present chapter proposes that teachers have partly appropriated the notion that parents are not to be held responsible for their child's achievements; the teachers affirm the notion that they themselves have great responsibility not only for the children but also for the parents. This is not to deny that parental involvement and good parenthood are also connected to middle-class parenting, as previous studies have stated (for example, Lareau 2000, 2011; Reay 2004). Children who grow up in families with financial resources and cultural capital that facilitate an auspicious home-learning environment have greater chances of school success: the teachers' definitions of good parenthood and parental involvement are certainly also informed by this reality.

The meaning of good parenthood is situated and dynamic; it evolves from negotiations between teachers and parents at a particular school. However, these negotiations are interlaced not only with national and local policies but also with political resource allocation and school leadership. It must be acknowledged that parents and teachers in disadvantaged areas face specific challenges that influence home-school relations (Bergnehr 2012, 2016). This study indicates that mediating teachers provide important support for the classroom teachers as well as for children and parents. They inform parents of the schooling system, and they interpret communication between parents and teachers on an everyday basis. As such, their work has the potential to encourage parental involvement and benefit home-school relations. These mediating teachers were introduced into the school due to a successful project that was running in the local authority where the data were collected. It appears that mediating teachers benefit schooling, teaching and home-school relations, and could do so in other municipalities as well.

NOTE

1. The data collection was funded by the Swedish National Institute of Public Health. The author wishes to thank the teachers who took part in the study.

REFERENCES

Baez, B., and S. Talburt. 2008. "Governing for responsibility and with love: Parents and children between home and school". *Educational Theory* 58(1): 25–43.

Bergnehr, D. 2012. "Barnet, hemmet och skolan i ett socioekonomiskt utsatt bostadsområde". In *Familjeliv och lärande* [Family life and learning], edited by L. Aarsand and P. Aarsand, 87–103. Lund: Studentlitteratur.

Bergnehr, D. 2015a. "Advancing home-school relations through parent support?". *Ethnography and Education* 10(2): 170–184.

Bergnehr, D. 2015b. "Föräldrastöd genom skolan: Diskursiva tillämpningar av nationell politik inom en svensk kommun". *Nordic Studies in Education* 35(1): 70–83.

Bergnehr, D. 2016. "Mothering for discipline and educational success: Welfare-reliant immigrant women talk about motherhood in Sweden". *Women's Studies International Forum* 54: 29–37.

Bergnehr, D., and K. Zetterqvist Nelson. 2015. "Where is the child? A discursive exploration of the positioning of children in research on mental-health-promoting interventions". *Sociology of Health and Illness* 37(2): 184–197.

Bouakaz, L. 2008. *Föräldrasamverkan i mångkulturella skolor*. Lund: Studentlitteratur.

Bridges, D. 2008. "Educationalization: On the appropriateness of asking educational institutions to solve social and economic problems". *Educational Theory* 58(4): 461–474.

Coffey, A. 2001. *Education and social change*. Buckingham: Open University Press.

Crozier, G. 1998. "Parents and schools: Partnership or surveillance?". *Journal of Education Policy* 13(1): 125–136.

Crozier, G., and J. Davies. 2007. "Hard to reach parents or hard to reach schools? A discussion of home-school relations, with particular reference to Bangladeshi and Pakistani parents". *British Educational Research Journal* 33(3): 295–313.

Dahlstedt, M., and F. Hertzberg. 2011. *Skola i samverkan: Miljonprogrammet och visionen om den öppna skolan.* Malmö: Gleerups.

Edwards, R. 2002. *Children, home and school.* New York: Routledge.

Lareau, A. 2000. *Home advantage: Social class and parental intervention in elementary education.* Lanham: Rowman & Littlefield Publishers.

Lareau, A. 2011. *Unequal childhoods: Class, race, and family life.* 2nd edition. Berkeley: University of California Press.

López, G. R., J.D. Scribner, and K. Mahitivanichcha. 2001. "Redefining parental involvement: Lessons from high-performing migrant-impacted schools". *American Educational Research Journal* 38(2): 253–288.

Reay, D. 2004. "Education and cultural capital: The implications of changing trends in education policies". *Cultural Trends* 13(2): 73–86.

Skolverket [The National Agency for Education]. 2009. *What influences educational achievement in Swedish schools?* Stockholm: Skolverket.

Statistics Sweden. 2007. *Children, segregated housing and school results: Demographic reports 2007:2.* Stockholm: Statistics Sweden.

Taylor, S. 2001. "Locating and conducting discourse analytic research". In *Discourse as data: A guide for analysis*, edited by M. Wetherell, S. Taylor and S.J. Yates, 5–48. London: Sage.

Van Den Berg, M., and R. Van Reekum. 2011. "Parent involvement as professionalization: Professionals' struggle for power in Dutch urban deprived areas.". *Journal of Education Policy* 26(3): 415–430.

Wells, M.B., and D. Bergnehr. 2014. "Family and family policies in Sweden". In *Handbook of family policies across the globe*, edited by M. Robila, 91–107). New York: Springer.

Woods, P, and M. Hammersley. 1993. *Gender and ethnicity in schools.* London: Routledge.

Disa Bergnehr, Ph.D., is Associate Professor in Child Studies and works at the School of Health and Welfare, Jönköping University, Sweden. Her current research interests are immigrant parenthood and family life, schooling and parenting in disadvantaged areas, school–home relations, children's health and well-being, parent support policies and services, and children's socialisation in preschools and families.

CHAPTER 8

Doing Good Parenthood Through Online Parental Involvement in Danish Schools

Maria Ørskov Akselvoll

Abstract In Denmark, involvement in children's schooling has become an integrated part of contemporary parenthood, during the last 30–40 years. For parents, this involves keeping up to date with daily classroom activities through the schools' Internet-based communication system, known as 'Parent Intranet'. This chapter investigates how two schools involve parents through Parent Intranet, examining how parents experience and deal with its online, omnipresent demands and expectations concerning involvement. Based on observations of the communication from the schools to the parents and semi-structured interviews with the parents, a Bourdieusian analysis of the parental perspective is carried out. The analysis focuses on the terms and conditions under which the two schools involved the parents. The study shows how the schools' digital efforts to involve parents implicitly required parents to continually be at the school's disposal, willing and able to closely follow and assist with their children's schooling. This chapter discusses how this results in the school acting as a gatekeeper for *doing good parenthood*.

Keywords Home-school cooperation · Parental involvement · Cultural capital · Parenting ideals · Intensive parenting · Parent Intranet

M.Ø. Akselvoll (✉)
Center for Childhood, Youth & Family Research, Department of People
& Technology, Roskilde University, Roskilde, Denmark
e-mail: mariaaks@ruc.dk

© The Author(s) 2016
A. Sparrman et al. (eds.), *Doing Good Parenthood*, Palgrave Macmillan
Studies in Family and Intimate Life, DOI 10.1007/978-3-319-46774-0_8

89

During the last 30–40 years, the home-school relationship in Denmark has intensified, primarily manifested as increased expectations and demands from schools on parental involvement in a wide variety of aspects of children's schooling. Researchers emphasise a high degree of parental involvement and more cooperation between home and school as a decisive factor for children's academic achievements (e.g. Desforges 2003; Epstein 2001), but also political emphasis has been put on this issue, partly fuelled by the increased focus on global competition and the survival of the welfare state (Pedersen 2011). As such, increased parental involvement has become a cultural truism, wiping away boundaries between school and family life, and inserting itself as an everyday activity in a Danish context (Dannesboe et al. 2012; Dannesboe 2013). For parents, this activity involves keeping up to date with their child's daily classroom activities through the school's online communication system, known as 'Parent Intranet'. Introduced in 2002, the Parent Intranet is currently being used by nearly all public schools in Denmark as the primary channel of communication between the school and the home. Parent Intranet is a part of School Intranet, a communications system for teachers, students and parents supervised by the National Agency for IT and Learning (STIL, stil.dk), a subdivision of the Ministry of Education. In 2014, a private company called *Itslearning* (itslearning.dk) took over the operation of School Intranet and it is planning to upgrade the system, which will enable schools to share more information with parents.

The questions are, how do different parents juggle the school's digital demands, and what does parental involvement mean to them in terms of being good parents? This chapter addresses these questions through a theoretical lens of differences. Working with Pierre Bourdieu's theory of the educational system and institutional reproduction (Bourdieu and Passeron 1970) and his concepts of field and capital (Bourdieu 1984, 2007), the analysis focuses on the terms under which parents are being involved by the school and on how different parents, equipped with various resources, meet and deal with these terms. Following Bourdieu, I view the school as a structured social field with a particular set of logics that attribute value to specific kinds of knowledge and certain ways of acting, instead of others. Of particular value in the school field is cultural capital, which is the knowledge and practical sense of society's legitimate culture and thus also academic culture (Bourdieu and Passeron 1970). In this particular case, especially with regard to the parents' educational background, occupational status, and the academic and practical skills that come with both, well-educated parents are in a position to place their child and themselves advantageously in the school system (see Bæck 2010; Lareau 2011; Reay 1998). The school field is not an isolated field though, but rather one that exchanges logics with other social fields – such as the field of parenthood, where the dominant ideal today is that of intensive parenting, which means a child-centred family life characterised by a particularly labour-intensive parenting style that emphasises learning, development and the avoidance of risk (Furedi 2008; Lee 2014). This is a societal ideal that all parents must relate to, as Stefansen (2011) points out, but one that presupposes middle-class resources, cultural as well as material (Faircloth 2014).

The analysis will show how this logic works when schools involve parents via digital means. I will explore how parents *do* parenthood with Parent Intranet as a platform and through this I will uncover how Parent Intranet works in the construction of the good parenthood.

The Study

This chapter presents and discusses findings from a qualitative research project on parental involvement in schooling, focusing on how schools use Parent Intranet to involve parents in their children's schooling and what using Parent Intranet means to different parents (Akselvoll, Forthcoming). The data, gathered as part of my Ph.D., also comprises records documenting the frequency of the parents' monthly logins to Parent Intranet, two teacher interviews, the observations of 91 parent-teacher conferences, two parent meetings and of two social events at the schools, but this article draws mainly on the observations of, and documents from, Parent Intranet and the interviews with parents. The research study examines parental involvement at two schools in central Copenhagen over the course of the 2013–2014 academic year. I conducted virtual observations of Parent Intranet for two primary school classes, which involved registering information from the school and collecting various electronic documents in order to analyse the school's requirements and expectations towards parents. Furthermore, I interviewed 20 parents from different socio-economic backgrounds, exploring their involvement in the school and their use of Parent Intranet. This chapter highlights and contrasts two cases on two different mothers in the study. With inspiration from Bourdieu (1999), the purpose of choosing two very different cases is to expand the differences in parental involvement and its role in parenting. There were many variations in between these two *extremes*, as well. These two particular cases were selected because they serve to magnify the main issue of interest: the different ways in which parents experience and deal with the efforts of schools to involve them, and how Parent Intranet becomes a platform for doing good parenthood.

DIGITAL INVOLVEMENT OF PARENTS

Parent Intra is used for all communication between the home and the school from the child's first day of school. Parents receive e-mail notifications whenever something new is posted on Parent Intranet, primarily information from the head of the school, school staff, and the teachers. Likewise, parents can contact the school through Parent Intranet, where all practical information about the school and the individual class is available. Parents can also communicate with each other through the system.

The schools in this study use Parent Intranet as a means to inform parents and to involve them in their children's schooling. For example, parents are asked to help their children with assignments and to oversee their children's reading. They also receive information about how to support their children's learning and they receive encouragement to engage in extra-curricular educational activities with their children. If a child forgets to do homework or hand in an assignment, teachers can also notify parents via Parent Intranet. Teachers involve parents as assistant teachers, supplying them with a steady stream of information to digest and act upon during the week. At the end of each week, teachers always send out 'the weekly schedule', which comprise a detailed weekly plan that inform parents about the upcoming week's activities, lists homework assignments with book and page references. On average (over the whole school year), parents received four messages weekly from Parent Intranet, such as newsletters from the teachers, information about upcoming fieldtrips, invitations to meetings or social events, links to educational websites, homework assignments, photos from school workshops and reminders. Most weeks deviate somewhat from the formal schedule in the sense that there are special activities on the agenda, for example, theme weeks or spontaneous fieldtrips. As such, Parent Intranet has a built-in, unpredictable aspect that requires parents to keep up with the news to avoid sending their children to school unprepared. Parent Intranet, thus, gives the teachers online access to parents, making it possible to involve parents at all times.

Parental Involvement through Parent Intranet

The parents, on the other hand, use Parent Intranet as a practical tool primarily to help their child be prepared for class. Parents use laptops and desktop computers, tablets as well as smartphones. They access Parent Intranet at home, at work or elsewhere and often check the weekly schedule for information about homework assignments and to learn if their child has done the homework. Parents are also expected to prepare their child mentally for class by telling the child about what is going to happen in school according to the weekly schedule. This entails logging in to Parent Intranet regularly to see what is new or if there are any changes and, as a minimum, reading the weekly schedule before the beginning of each new school week.

The common way for parents to use Parent Intranet is to keep up with news from the school management, the school board, the teachers and the social committee. Parents also use Parent Intranet to register for parent meetings, parent-teacher conferences and social events. However, parents also use the platform to plan birthday parties, camping trips, coordinate play dates, and exchange comments and opinions on all these matters.

There are, however, important differences in how parents use Parent Intranet and the degree to which they keep up with it. Some parents log on to Parent Intranet twice a day, others twice a week, while others rarely use it. It also varies how much attention is paid to detail. Some parents make a strong effort to comply with every single call for involvement, while others take a more relaxed approach, seeking to pick out what they find most important. Some parents have a highly organised way of handling Parent Intranet that involves printing out the weekly schedule, putting it up on the fridge and updating their electronic agendas to remind themselves of special events. Others are less structured and check Parent Intranet much less regularly, depending on the amount of other daily family life activities. Also, the task of keeping up with Parent Intranet falls mainly on the mothers, particularly in nuclear families. The fathers' use of Parent Intranet is, in most cases, a supplement to the mothers' use of it. When parents are divorced and the children stay with each parent every other week, the parents share the task of keeping up with Parent Intranet more evenly, as this living kind of arrangement makes it necessary for both parents to use it.

It follows from this that parental attitudes towards Parent Intranet also varies greatly, some seeing it as a helping hand and others viewing it as a burden. Many parents have ambivalent feelings as they find it to be a valuable tool, but one that is also time consuming and a source of everyday stress. Hence, Parent Intranet has very different meanings for parents, playing differently into their everyday lives, as the following cases on two mothers will show.

ACTIVATING RESOURCES, FEELING COMPETENT

Annette, 45, is the mother of two, works as a human resources executive and is married to Jens, who also holds a senior executive position. They both have high incomes and the family lives in a large apartment in an exclusive area of the city. The class teacher describes Annette as highly involved. She is an active member of the social committee and the family attends all school social events. During our interview, when asked about the first thing that came to mind when I said the term "Parent Intranet" she responded enthusiastically:

> Annette: Well, I'd say that I couldn't live without it [...] I log in every day to see what's happening in there. I think it's really good that we get all the information in one place... I use it a lot, just checking the front page, and whatever comes up there [...] And then there's the weekly schedule. I'm constantly keeping up with that.

Using a professional approach to handling Parent Intranet, Annette has established a regular routine, logging in at the same time each evening. In this way, she makes sure not to miss out on anything in case the teachers post a message late in the day. She always makes sure that she has enough time available to follow up instantly on whatever needs a response to avoid forgetting about it later on. She uses the weekly schedule to assist with her son Christian's learning. She uses the text book pages specified to help her to go through his books and to ask him relevant questions when they do homework together. Having in-depth knowledge of Christian's different skills, she actively seeks to improve his performance, using a variety of pedagogical techniques. She often does exercises with him that involve his weak spot – spelling – and he reads aloud to her almost daily.

Annette thinks that being involved in her son's schooling, actively seeking to comply with all of the school's demands and expectations, and wanting, as she explains, to "put in an extra effort" are naturally her responsibility as a parent. She admits that this is labour intensive, but she says, "I really like getting myself involved in activities related to his school". Navigating the school field is something she feels capable of and masters well, but it is also a source of satisfaction and enjoyment for her. Annette prioritises it highly, even with a demanding job and a busy lifestyle. Parental involvement, in other words, is a form of good parenthood to her.

Her involvement is thus intensive and characterised by being alert to the school's demands and constantly overseeing of her son's academic development. Like other parents in the study who are well endowed with cultural capital, education plays a central role in the family and the presence of Parent Intranet represents a means to strengthen Christian's academic achievements and to cooperate with the teachers to accomplish this.

FEELING LIKE A BAD MOTHER

A boy named Simon is in the same class as Christian. His mother, Heidi, 29, has three children. Her boyfriend is the father of Christian's younger siblings, but Heidi and her boyfriend do not live together. She has been unemployed for a long time and is on the dole, receiving security provisions. The family lives in a small flat in publically funded housing. The class teacher describes Heidi as "the young mum", criticising her for not using Parent Intranet enough. She is not very active socially in school, attending only a few social events. At our interview, when asked about the first thing that came to her mind when I said the term "Parent Intranet", she responded promptly:

> Heidi: I hate it! Hate it! [. . .] The whole thing, us parents having to check it – sometimes every day because sometimes the teacher will post a message at nine in the evening. A message needed for the next day. And I've already checked it at four in the afternoon. I'm not checking it twice a day!

Unlike Annette, Heidi has not developed an organised Parent Intranet routine. She is not as structured about logging in. Sometimes she acts on the information and sometimes she does not. Since she is unsure of when the teachers will send out information, she thinks that Parent Intranet is unpredictable, which makes her feel anxious and overwhelmed by its omnipresence. She does not have a computer and finds the interface messy and complicated on her small smartphone screen. No printing options are available and she would prefer it if the teacher could just give her a piece of paper instead. Fully aware that she is expected to log in to Parent Intranet more often than she does, she still resists:

> Heidi: […] it irritates me, the feeling of being a bad mother if you don't do all the things they want you to do. I think that's just wrong. I'm not the one who's in school. Simon is the one who's in school. I'm here for him when he has homework to do; I'm here when he wants to ask me something. I'm there for the school meetings and the Christmas party and stuff like that. But really, spending fifteen to twenty minutes each night trying to figure out your way around Parent Intranet is just too much, if you ask me.

Not complying completely with the school's demands is a way for Heidi to keep the school at a distance. However, the constant presence of Parent Intranet makes it difficult to do just that. So she also makes an effort to improve and to log in to Parent Intranet more often, especially after a parent-teacher conference, when she learns, to her surprise, that Simon is lagging behind due to her lack of involvement. She finds that not doing "all the things they want you to do" is simply wrong when it makes her feel like a "bad mother". To Heidi, good parenthood is not necessarily about being involved in school but about being there for Simon, if and when he needs her. In stressing that "**Simon** is the one who's in school", and not her, she puts a limit on the level of her involvement, drawing a line between her parental responsibility and the responsibility of the school.

Heidi feels that the school interferes with family life, exceeding what she finds acceptable. It also exceeds what she feels capable of. She is unsure of how to use the information in the weekly schedule since she is "not educated as a teacher or anything". With only a high school diploma and little experience in the labour market, she lacks cultural capital and the various skills it generates, in contrast to Annette, who can draw on those skills to handle Parent Intranet.

Resistance towards the school's demands and expectations characterises Heidi's limited involvement. She attempts to keep the school at a distance by *partly* ignoring the information in Parent Intranet, thus resulting in a discrepancy between knowing what the school expects of her and not satisfactorily meeting those expectations.

SAME DEMANDS – DIFFERENT PARENTS

How these two mothers experienced and handled the school's efforts to involve them is a reflection of what the school recognised as the ideal school parent, namely someone who personally takes on the responsibility of their child succeeding at school, is available and alert to the school's expectations, and who is willing and able to constantly oversee and assist with learning and homework. In other words, the school's intensified efforts to involve parents operated according to an intensive parenting ideal of "ever-present, constantly attuned parents" (Faircloth 2014, 30) who devote large amounts of time and energy to their child. This parenting ideal is typically valued and practiced by middle and upper-middle-class parents (Forsberg 2009; Gillies 2005; Lareau 2000, 2011; Nelson 2010; Vincent and Ball 2007), who by means of their access to cultural capital are also especially capable of assisting in their children's education. Like Annette, the other well-educated parents in this study involved themselves according to an intensive parenting logic, viewing their involvement in school as an important parental responsibility. In contrast, Heidi and the other parents in the study who were less able to activate cultural capital set clearer boundaries for the school's presence in their family life, practiced school involvement in a less organised way and also distanced themselves during interviews from the highly involved parents in the class, stressing other less performance-oriented activities as important parental responsibilities. Their ideals concerning good parenthood were defined more according to what Lareau (2011, 3) terms "the accomplishment of natural growth", letting the child develop at its own pace – as opposed to supervising and cultivating it. According to Nelson (2010), this less-intensive style allows working-class parents to experience fewer internal contradictions in their parenting approach compared to upper-middle-class parents. Heidi, however, was torn between the two contradictory ideals, leaning towards a natural growth style of parenthood, but finding that she does not measure up when comparing herself against the ideal of intensive parenthood. This meant that Heidi assessed her parenting according to the ambivalent ideal of relaxed intensiveness while simultaneously rejecting the school's agenda *and* attempting to incorporate it, causing her to feel pressured and inadequate as a parent.

CONCLUDING DISCUSSION

As the above discussion shows, the schools' efforts to involve parents digitally created a framework where keeping up and being deeply involved in their child's schooling involves not only supporting one's child but also negotiating what good parenting is in relationship to the intensive ideal. Parents with different socio-economic backgrounds, however, navigate differently within this framework, as the chapter has demonstrated. For some, parental involvement can be a way of doing good parenthood since the expectation of the schools concerning involvement corresponds well with their own ideal, practice and competencies. For others, it serves as a complicating barrier that requires too many resources, creating a constant conflict between the schools' version of good parenthood and the parents' own. For everyone, the desire to be a good parent is strong and a large amount of work – practical and emotional – is involved.

With the increased efforts of schools to involve parents through digital communication and the responsibility it subsequently assigns parents, it can be argued that access to doing good parenthood in the field of the school is increasingly dependent on opportunities for activating cultural capital, as well as ascribing to the right parenthood ideal.

REFERENCES

Akselvoll, M.Ø. 2015. "Det digitaliserede skole-hjem samarbejde i et forældreperspektiv – om forældres forskellige involveringsstrategier på Forældreintra" [Digital Home-School Collaboration from Parents' Perspective – Parents' Different Strategies of Digital Involvement in School]. *Dansk Pædagogisk Tidsskrift* 4: 25–33.

Akselvoll, M.Ø. Forthcoming. *Folkeskole, forældre, forskelle. Skole-hjem-samarbejde og forældreinvolvering i et klasseperspektiv [School, parents, differences. Home-school cooperation and parental involvement in a class perspective].* Ph.D. thesis, Department of People and Technology, Roskilde: Roskilde University.

Bæck, U.-D.K. 2010. "Parental involvement practices in formalized home-school cooperation." *Scandinavian Journal of Educational Research* 54: 549–563.

Bourdieu, P. 1984. *Distinction*. London: Routledge.

Bourdieu, P. 1999. *Den maskuline dominans [Masculine Domination]*. København: Tiderne skifter.

Bourdieu, P. 2007. *Den praktiske sans [The Logic of Practice]*. Copenhagen: Hans Reitzel Publishers.

Bourdieu, P., and J.C. Passeron. 1970. *Reproduktionen. Bidrag til en teori om undervisningssystemet [Reproduction in Education, Society and Culture]*. Copenhagen: Hans Reitzel Publishers.

Dannesboe, K.I. 2013. "Den grænseløse skole?" [The limitless school?]. *Barn* 4: 45–60.

Dannesboe, K.I., N. Kryger, C. Palludan, and B. Ravn. 2012. *Hvem sagde samarbejde? Et hverdagslivsstudie af skole-hjem-relationer [Who said cooperation? A study of home-school relations in everyday life]*. Aarhus: Aarhus Universitetsforlag.

Desforges, C., and A. Abouchaar. 2003. *The impact of parental involvement, parental support and family education on pupil achievements and adjustment: A literature review.* Research Report RR433, Department for Education and Skills, United Kingdom.

Epstein, J.L. 2001. *School, family and community partnership: Preparing educators and improving schools.* Boulder: Westview Press.

Faircloth, C. (2014). "Intensive parenting and the expansion of parenting." In *Parenting culture studies,* edited by E. Lee, J. Bristow, C. Faircloth, and J. Macvarish, 25–50. Basingstoke: Palgrave MacMillan.

Forsberg, L. 2009. *Involved parenthood: Everyday lives of Swedish middle-class families.* Ph.D. thesis, Department of Thematic Studies – Child Studies. Linköping: Linköping University.

Furedi, F. 2008. *Paranoid parenting.* London: Continuum.

Gillies, V. 2005. "Raising the 'meritocracy': Parenting and the individualization of social class." *Sociology* 39: 835–863.

Lareau, A. 2000. *Home advantage: Social class and parental intervention in elementary education.* Langham: Rowman & Littlefield.

Lareau, A. 2011. *Unequal childhoods: Class, race and family life.* Berkeley: University of California Press.

Lee, E. (2014). Introduction. In *Parenting culture studies,* edited by E. Lee, J. Bristow, C. Faircloth and J. Macvarish, 1–22. Basingstoke: Palgrave Macmillan.

Nelson, M.K. 2010. *Parenting out of control.* New York: New York University Press.

Pedersen, O.K. 2011. *Konkurrencestaten [The competition state].* Copenhagen: Hans Reitzel Publishers.

Reay, D. (1998). "Cultural reproduction: Mothers' involvement in their children's primary schooling." In *Bourdieu and education,* edited by M. Grenfell and D. James, 55–70. London: Palmer Press.

Stefansen, K. 2011. *Foreldreskap i småbarnsfamilien: Klassekultur og sosial reproduksjon [Parenthood in families with young children: Class culture and social reproduction].* Ph.D. thesis, Department of Sociology and Human Geography. Oslo: University of Oslo.

Vincent, C., and S.J. Ball. 2007. "'Making up' the middle-class child: Families, activities and class dispositions." *Sociology* 41: 1061–1077.

Maria Ørskov Akselvoll is a sociologist and a Ph.D. student at the Department of People & Technology, Roskilde University, Denmark. Her research areas cover parental involvement in schools, parenthood, family life and social class. Of particular interest, and the topic of her forthcoming thesis, are the inter-institutional connections between schools' demands and expectations of parental involvement, and parents' different everyday lives and resources.

CHAPTER 9

Teenagers, Alcohol and Sex: Doing Good Parenthood on an On-line Discussion Board

Judith Lind

Abstract Teenagers, sex and alcohol are frequent topics on an on-line discussion board for Swedish parents. The aim of this study is to analyse how the posters to the discussion board do good parenthood by discussing parental strategies in relation to teenagers, alcohol and sex. The topics of alcohol and sex are chosen because they serve well to address the tension between a teenager's entitlement to autonomy over decisions concerning her/his own body and parents' responsibility for ensuring the well-being and socialisation of their child. The analysis shows that, despite considerable differences in the parenting strategies proposed by posters, there are two overarching ideals for good parenthood: the ideal of not taking the easy route as a parent and the ideal of the well-being of the teenager as the primary concern when placing restrictions on teenagers' behaviour.

Keywords On-line discussion · Teenagers · Sex · Alcohol

J. Lind (✉)
Department of Thematic Studies – Child Studies, Linköping University,
Linköping, Sweden
e-mail: judith.lind@liu.se

© The Author(s) 2016
A. Sparrman et al. (eds.), *Doing Good Parenthood*, Palgrave Macmillan
Studies in Family and Intimate Life, DOI 10.1007/978-3-319-46774-0_9

101

The parenting style that is most often favoured in parent education programmes, explicitly or implicitly, is an authoritative parenting style, sometimes called "assertive democratic" (Ramaekers and Suissa 2012) or active parenting. It values autonomous self-will as well as disciplined conformity, exerts control without hemming the child and requires parents to strike a balance in order to be not too permissive and not too restrictive or controlling. It is one of three parenting styles originally identified by Diana Baumrind (1966, 1967): "authoritarian", "authoritative" and "permissive". Whereas the permissive parenting style is described as non-punitive and as making few demands for household responsibility and orderly behaviour, the authoritarian parent is said to control the child in accordance with a set standard of conduct, to value obedience and restrict the child's autonomy (Baumrind 1967). The authoritative parenting style is portrayed as a balanced middle way. It is also a parenting style that emphasises the need for parents to be active, rather than passive, and to be involved and emotionally close; and it demands that parents be willing to invest both time and energy in their parenting task (Wissö 2012). It has been associated with ideologies of "intensive mothering" (Hays 1996) or "involved parenthood" (Forsberg 2009), places the child at the centre of family life and requests parents to be emotionally close to their children as well as to set limits and rules for them (Böök and Perälä-Littunen 2008; Dahl 2014).

The exerting of parental control, the setting of rules and parental involvement all presuppose parents' rights to intervene in their children's lives. Focusing on the parents of teenagers, this article examines a phase in parenthood, and childhood, during which such a right can be seen as decreasingly self-evident. Satu Perälä-Littunen and Marja Leena Böök (2012) note that the parents in their study described parental responsibility in terms of the right to interfere in their child's life and that this right ends when responsibility ends. An interesting question is therefore how parents justify their interference in their teenagers' lives at a point in time when their responsibility, and therefore their right to interfere, is about to end.

The data that is used for the study consists of posts made to the on-line discussion board on the Swedish website *Familjeliv.se* [Family Life] The aim of the article is to analyse how posters on the discussion board do good parenthood: how they position themselves and other posters as good, or not so good, parents when they discuss teenagers, alcohol and sex, and how they thereby contribute to construing and negotiating definitions of good parenthood.

Why Alcohol and Sex?

Opening posts indicate that the teenage children of posters are engaged in or want to engage in a range of activities that parents do not necessarily approve of. These activities include, amongst others, the consumption of alcohol and sexual activities. I have chosen the topics of alcohol and sex because both of them concern the body of the teenager. They, therefore, serve well to address the tension between the teenager's entitlement to autonomy over decisions concerning her/his own body, on one hand, and parents' responsibility for ensuring the physical safety and well-being of their child, on the other. However, alcohol and sex also differ slightly in terms of the degree of harmfulness that is associated with them by parents in Sweden. Parents' standpoints with regard to their teenagers' sexual behaviour tend, as we will see, to be more complex. Although a general goal for parenting related to these issues may be described as encouraging a balanced and healthy relationship to alcohol and sex, the preferred outcome regarding the consumption of alcohol comes closer to complete abstinence than does the preferred outcome of parenting regarding sex. This also indicates that the strategies put forward by parents on the board regarding their teenagers' drinking and sexual behaviour are informed not only by considerations of their effects on the teenagers' well-being, but also, to some extent, by social norms and standards of conduct as well as the extent to which parents believe that they can and should control their teenagers' behaviour (Lind 2016 forthcoming).

The Study

In contrast to interviews, posts to on-line discussion boards constitute naturally occurring data, that is spontaneous utterances on subjects initiated by the poster her/himself (Robinson 2001) or simply posters' everyday talk (Callaghan and Lazard 2012; See also Alstam 2013; Russell 2012). When parents give each other advice on discussion boards, they simultaneously argue in favour of a particular parenting behaviour and they frequently do so by describing their own strategies and choices in similar situations. Therefore, posts to on-line discussion boards serve well as data for an analysis of how parents position themselves and others in relation to definitions of good parenting and how they reproduce or negotiate these (Mungham and Lazard 2011).

Familjeliv.se introduces itself as a meeting place on the web that was started by parents in 2003 in order to be able "to meet and receive advice, support and help regarding the family, parenthood and pregnancy in a social network" (my translation). It claims to have 780,000 unique visitors each week and to be visited by half of all mothers in Sweden with children aged 0–6 (www.familjeliv.se/article/Information/om (140827)). The posts that were selected for the present analysis were made in the discussion group for parents of teenagers on the general parent discussion board. Between 30/08/2009 and 30/08/2012, a total of 594 discussion threads were started or responded to in this discussion group. For this analysis, I selected all threads that concerned alcohol (21 threads comprising 519 posts) and sexuality (24 threads comprising 888 posts). All quotations from posts and discussion thread headlines have been translated by me.

Ethical Considerations

Posts to on-line discussion boards are made independently and without the knowledge of the research that uses it as data, which raises questions concerning informed consent. Researchers have made a distinction between discussion boards and chat rooms that are password protected and to which access is restricted through requirements of membership, on one hand, and discussion boards on which posts are open for anybody to read, on the other. Whereas participants on password-protected discussion boards have the right to assume that their posts will not be read by anyone outside of that particular board's on-line community, posters on open-access boards can be expected to realise that their posts, similar to blog entries or other digitally published material, can be read by anyone (Markham 2005; Robinson 2001). Since the posts made on the discussion boards at *Familjeliv.se* are public and can be read by anyone, consent has not been sought.

Gender and Age

Good parenthood is not the same for mothers and fathers (Walzer 1998). Neither are the expectations of parents of boys and parents of girls necessarily the same. This may be particularly true with regard to matters concerning alcohol and sex. Similarly, discussions on where to draw the line between harmful and non-harmful behaviours and on teenagers' right to privacy as a limitation on parents' rights to intervene are likely to be affected by the discussed teenager's gender and age. The on-line discussion board as data source here poses a problem. The poster's gender is seldom disclosed in the posts. The gender of the teenager that an opening post concerns is disclosed more often. In the opening posts of the 21 threads on alcohol, the teenagers referred to are boys in five cases and girls in 13 cases, whereas the remaining three opening post concern teenagers in general. In the opening posts of the 24 threads on sexuality, the teenagers are boys in nine cases, girls in 11 cases and teenagers in general in four cases. An analysis of whether and how parenting ideals differ with the age and gender of the child has the potential to contribute further knowledge on parents' negotiations of parenting ideals, but falls outside the scope of this chapter.

Themes

All discussion threads have been analysed thematically (Clarke and Braun 2006; Clarke et al. 2014). After the threads had been read and reread, initial codes were generated (alcohol: buying alcohol, serving alcohol and teenagers' consumption of alcohol; sexuality: under-aged teenagers and sex, promiscuity). In the next stage of the analysis, codes were collated into two preliminary themes: the *concerns* that parents addressed in their posts and the *advice* that was given to parents. Broadly, posts can be categorised in terms of the extent to which parents are seen as able and obliged to intervene and regulate their teenagers' drinking and sexual behaviour. Five categories of parental strategies advocating varying degrees of parental intervention were generated, referring to the differences between various parental approaches and how they are justified. Five quotes taken from discussion board posts serve to illustrate these strategies: "You're the parent and you're responsible...", "Let her learn from her mistakes", "We opt for damage control", "Don't preach about right and wrong, just talk...", and "It's none of your business". Whereas the first four standpoints were represented in posts about alcohol as well as sex, the fifth was only found in relation to the sexual behaviour of teenagers. It demands a limitation on parents' regulation of their teenagers' lives, not primarily out of consideration for how parents can achieve a preferred outcome but because parents do not have the right to interfere in their teenagers' sexual lives.

Interestingly, it is not necessarily the poster's standpoint as such that decides how a post is received by other participants but rather the quality of the argumentation. Posters can, for example, very well state that they do not control their teenager's drinking and that they are even prepared to serve alcohol to their teenager and still be awarded the status of a responsible and good parent. Two overarching parenthood ideals that cut across all differences were identified: the ideal of not taking the easy route and the ideal of making the teenager's well-being the foremost concern. In this chapter, I have selected four discussion threads to illustrate these two ideals.

NOT TAKING THE EASY ROUTE

In one opening post, the poster, who introduces himself as a single father of an almost 13-year-old girl, asks for advice on a range of topics, including the consumption of alcohol ("13-year-old daughter – what rules for alcohol, parties, computer, clothes and curfews?" 24/11/2011, read 8908 times, 95 replies). The poster writes that he has served wine and cider to his daughter and that he has let her take alcohol with her to parties. Although the opening poster's (hereafter op) way of reasoning resembles other posters' standpoints – he thinks it is safer if his daughter drinks wine that he has bought rather than illicitly distilled alcohol of unknown origin and he wants to safeguard his close relationship with his daughter – several factors led to his reasoning being seen as unacceptable. Some posters found the op's standpoint so controversial that they questioned his authenticity and accused him of being a "troll" (24/11/2011, #20, 58). First of all, the child in question is much younger than the teenagers who are discussed in other threads concerning alcohol. Furthermore, his view on alcohol is regarded as very liberal; he not only accepts that his daughter drinks, but he offers her alcohol and even buys alcohol for consumption elsewhere. Furthermore, in contrast to many other posters, this op is not explicit about how he believes that his parenting strategies contribute to limiting the risks that may be associated with his daughter's drinking.

This differentiates his post from another opening post provocatively labelled "Why I would treat a 15-year-old to one hell of a booze-up" (17/12/2009, read 2769 times, 26 replies). This op justifies her/his idea by saying that s/he wants her/his son to be in a safe environment when he first experiences the effects of being drunk and hopes that this experience, which the op envisions to include dizziness, vomiting and "a proper hangover", will cure his curiosity and give him a distaste for alcohol. Although many of the parents who replied to this post were sceptical of this strategy, the discussion tone in the thread was respectful and no suspicions of the op being a troll were expressed. What further distinguishes this opening post from the above is the op's demand in a later post for parents to take responsibility.

> Surely it's better to be realistic and realise that it may very well be that my children drink or try to get hold of alcohol or fags or whatever it might be, and instead of being blinkered about this fact, to simply open one's eyes and tackle the problem? To NOT think about alcohol and other drugs when you have children, is to not take responsibility, I think. (17/12/2009 #18).

The opening poster thereby positions her/himself against parents who remain passive in their approach to teenage drinking. The poster does not simply surrender to the wish of the 15-year-old son to drink alcohol but emphasises that s/he takes action. The poster thereby presents her/himself as a responsible parent, who does not shy away either from unconventional strategies or from sacrificing her/his own comfort in order to limit the son's drinking. The father of the 12-year-old girl also displays engagement with his daughter. He writes that he loves his daughter, that they are "friends as much as we are father and daughter" (24/11/2011, #40) and that he knows how much she likes to party. In this way, however, and in contrast to the op who wants to treat her/his son to a proper booze-up, he comes across as a parent who avoids conflict and seeks his daughter's approval and companionship rather than assuming responsibility for protecting her against something potentially harmful. One of the many upset reply posts targets just that.

> First of all, you are supposed to be her dad, not her friend as you write above. She has friends already, it's a DAD that she needs. Parents are for rules and for setting the boundaries that children that age do not set themselves. (24/11/2011, #50).

Hence, the reactions to the above two posts indicate that parents, in order to be acknowledged as good parents by other posters on the discussion board, are first and foremost expected to be active in their parenting and not to shy away from strategies that are demanding of the parent, either because they require the parent to enforce unpopular rules or because they are controversial and/or require the parent to invest time, and, in the second op's case, to also be willing to mop up their child's vomit.

Does this mean that involved, active or intense parenting is never criticised on the discussion board? No, the aims of parental rules and interventions as they are presented in these posts seem to be just as important for how a post is received. Intervention that is not primarily justified as serving to protect the teenager from potential harm or to further her/his well-being – immediate or future – but that is instead framed as a matter of morality or a way to influence the teenager's standard of conduct is at times subjected to criticism on the board.

MAKING THE TEENAGER'S WELL-BEING THE FOREMOST CONCERN

A discussion thread that illustrates this was started by the father of a 14-year-old boy. In his post, the father says that he has asked his son to only masturbate in the bathroom and only when no one else is at home. ("Have rules for masturbation?" 13/5/2012, read 17,681 times, 78 replies). The op justifies his restrictions by claiming that he wants to avoid stains on the sheets and by referring to a need to show consideration for other family members. The reactions to this post are fierce and this op too is suspected of being a troll. The overall message to the op is that his son's sex life is none of his business and that it is wrong to make his son feel guilty about masturbating.

> What the hell do you as dad have to do with his sexuality? Is it really the sperm that bothers you or the fact that he masturbates? (13/5/2012, #4)

A key aspect of this discussion thread is that the sexual behaviour under discussion is not considered by either the op or the response posters as harmful to the boy. Therefore, regulating it does not serve the purpose of protecting him. On the contrary, it is even seen by some of the response posters as detrimental to his development of a healthy sexuality.

Instead, the above-cited poster seems to suspect that the op is moralising over the activity as such, a suspicion that is confirmed when, later in the discussion, the op refers to masturbation as something "filthy" (13/5/2012, #22). The fierce reaction to the op illustrates that morality is not accepted on the discussion board as a valid argument. Such a conclusion is further supported by the discussion following an opening post concerning the sexual behaviour of another op's 14-year-old daughter ("My daughter, 14-year-old, sleeps around" 18/12/2010, read 11,392 times, 134 replies). According to the op, the girl has had sex with ten different partners in the last nine months, which is referred to by the op as sleeping around. The post ends with the following:

> When I explained to her that she would get a bad reputation amongst her friends if this continued, she became angry and went to her room. My daughter is 14 years old and has had sex with approximately 15 guys, this worries me enormously.... So the question now is, WHAT SHALL I DO?! (18/12/2010, opening post).

The op states as the reason for her concern her daughter's reputation. Throughout the discussion thread, she receives support for her standpoint that something needs to be done. However, a smaller number of posters instead advise the op that "there is probably not much she can do" (#23, 26, 38) or state that her daughter's sex life is none of her business (#35, 48). These posters accuse those who urge the op to intervene as acting out of moral panic.

Interestingly, those posters who agree that the op should intervene also distance themselves from any moral judgement of the girl's behaviour and from seeing the girl's reputation as grounds for action. Instead, they express concern about the reasons for her behaviour and for her mental well-being.

> To say that she should stop "sleeping around" because others will otherwise see her as bad is kind of the wrong way to go in all this, it's not because others are judgemental and condescending that a potentially destructive behaviour is bad. (18/12/2010, #51)

This discussion thread illustrates that references to morality, a certain standard of conduct, or concern about what others may think are not regarded on the discussion board as valid arguments for parental intervention regarding the sexual behaviour of a teenager. Hence, stopping a sexual behaviour in order to protect a teenager from something that is considered as harmful is positioned as good parenting, whereas doing the same thing in order to protect a moral standard, or adjust the teenager's morality, is not.

Concluding Discussion

On the discussion board, parents do good parenthood by promoting different parenting strategies in relation to teenagers, sex and alcohol and by positioning themselves and other posters in relation to these. The strategies range from regulating behaviours and setting limits to letting go and respecting the teenager's right to privacy. Despite these far-reaching differences, there are two overarching ideals that cut across all differences: the ideal of not taking the easy route as a parent, and the ideal of making the well-being of the teenager the primary concern in restricting the teenager's behaviour.

The first of these supports an ideal of intensive (Hays 1996), engaged (Sawyer 1999) or involved (Forsberg 2009), and to some extent sacrificial (Göknar 2013) parenthood, as noted in previous research. This ideal, as it finds expression in the on-line posts about teenagers' consumption of alcohol and sexual behaviour, is separated from posters' inclination to promote parental regulation of their teenagers' behaviour. Regardless of whether posters argued in favour of parental intervention or not, they strove to present themselves as being engaged and involved, and demanded that other posters also convey that they cared and were concerned with their teenager's well-being and safety.

The second ideal that emerges from the analysis of the on-line posts constitutes an additional dimension of what is seen as good parenthood. The ideal of making the well-being of the teenager the primary concern when restricting the teenager's behaviour indicates that, for parental intervention to be acknowledged as good parenting on the discussion board, it must be justified in a particular manner. According to this ideal, the purpose of any parental intervention in a teenager's life must be related to the safety or well-being, immediate or future, of the child in order to be accepted. Correspondingly, societal norms or moral standpoints are generally not seen on the discussion board as justifiable concerns, just as the teenager's behavioural compliance in accordance with these norms is not seen as a justifiable goal of parenting practices. This explains why the tolerance for parental intervention on the discussion board was considerably lower with regard to sexual behaviour than when it came to the consumption of alcohol.

It was generally seen as desirable on the discussion board if teenagers could refrain from drinking, although not all posters saw this as a realistic goal. Engagement in sexual activities, however, were not seen as harmful as such. There was concern about some sexual behaviours as indicators of mental health issues, as well as about the circumstances under which sex took place, which was expressed through posters' readiness to allow girlfriends or boyfriends to stay overnight and their desire to make their teenager feel comfortable when talking about sex with their parents. Thus, when the sexual behaviour as such was seen as non-detrimental to the teenager's physical or mental well-being, there was general agreement on the discussion board that parents had no right to interfere. Good parenthood was done by displaying care and concern for the well-being of the teenager and the discussion board served as a very suitable platform for this practice.

References

Alstam, K. 2013. "Ideologies of mothering in an internet forum: Hurting narratives and declarative defence." *Power and Education* 5(1): 38–51.

Baumrind, D. 1966. "Effects of authoritative parental control on child behavior." *Child Development* 37(4): 887–907.

Baumrind, D. 1967. "Child care practices anteceding three patterns of preschool behavior." *Genetic Psychology Monographs*, 75(1): 43–88.

Böök, M.-L., and S. Perälä-Littunen. 2008. "'Children need their parents more than a pizza in the fridge!' Parental responsibility in a Finnish newspaper." *Childhood* 15: 74–88.

Braun, V., V. Clarke, and G. Terry. 2014. "Thematic analysis." In *Qualitative research in clinical and health psychology*, edited by P. Rohleder and A. Lyons, 95–113. Basingstoke: Palgrave MacMillan.

Callaghan, J.E.M., and L. Lazard. 2012. "'Please don't put the whole dang thing out there!' A discursive analysis of internet discussions around infant feeding." *Psychology & Health* 27(8): 938–955.

Clarke, V., and V. Braun. 2006. "Using thematic analysis in psychology." *Qualitative Research in Psychology* 3(2): 77–101.

Dahl, K.M. 2014. *Frihed, lighed og fællesskab i teenagefamilien – sociologiske kategoriseringer af familiepraksis i børnenes teenageår samt analyser af årsager til og konsekvenser af familiers praksis*, Ph.D. thesis, Department of Sociology. Copenhagen: Copenhagen University.onsekvenser af familiers praksis

Forsberg, L. 2009. *Involved parenthood: Everyday lives of Swedish middle-class families*, Ph.D. thesis, Department of Thematic Studies – Child Studies. Linköping: Linköping University.

Göknar, A.M. 2013. "Sacrificial mothering of IVF-pursuing mothers in Turkey." In *Parenting in global perspective: Negotiating ideologies of kinship, self and politics*, edited by C. Faircloth, D.M. Hoffman, and L.L. Layne, 200–212. London: Routledge.

Hays, S. 1996. *The cultural contradictions of motherhood*. New Haven: Yale University Press.

Lind, J. 2016, forthcoming. "Between zero tolerance and damage control: Policy and parental strategies concerning teenagers and alcohol." *Families, Relationships and Societies*.

Markham, A.N. 2005. "The methods, politics and ethics of representation in online ethnography." In *The Sage handbook of qualitative research*, edited by N.K. Denzin and Y.S. Lincoln, 3rd edition, 793–818. Thousand Oaks: Sage.

Mungham, S., and L. Lazard. 2011. "Virtually experts: Exploring constructions of mothers' advice-seeking in online parenting communities." *Radical Psychology* 9(2).

Perälä-Littunen, S., and M.-L. Böök. 2012. "The beginning and end of parental responsibility: Finnish parents' views." *Journal of Comparative Family Studies* 43(6): 925–941.

Ramaekers, S., and J. Suissa. 2012. *The claims of parenting: Reasons, responsibility and society*. Dordrecht: Springer.

Robinson, K.M. 2001. "Unsolicited narratives from the Internet: A rich source of qualitative data." *Qualitative Health Research*, 11: 706–714.

Russell, S. 2012. "Social networking research opportunities: The example of 'Netmums'." *Journal of Research in Nursing*, 17(2): 195–206.

Sawyer, L.M. 1999. "Engaged mothering: The transition to motherhood for a group of African American women." *Journal of Transcultural Nursing* 10(1): 14–21.

Walzer, S. 1998. *Thinking about the baby: Gender and transition into parenthood*. Philadelphia: Temple University Press.

Wissö, T. 2012. *Småbarnsföräldrars vardagsliv. Omsorg, moral och social capital*, Ph.D. thesis, Department of Social Work. Gothenburg: Gothenburg University. www.familjeliv.se/article/Information/om (140827).

Judith Lind, Ph.D., is a lecturer at the Department of Thematic Studies – Child Studies, Linköping University, Sweden, where she is the director of the Master's and Ph.D. programmes in Child Studies. Her general research interests concern the relationships between parents, children and the state. She is currently involved in research projects on parental support, adoption, and assisted reproduction and has a particular interest in the vetting of would-be parents.

CHAPTER 10

The Ontological Choreography of (Good) Parenthood

Anna Sparrman, David Cardell, Anne-Li Lindgren
and Tobias Samuelsson

Abstract The aim of this study is to unpack the notion of family togetherness as constitutive of good parenthood during visits to child cultural establishments like amusement parks, theme parks and children's museums. The analyses challenge earlier assumptions of intensive family togetherness – such as closeness, spending time together and cohesion – by showing how togetherness is being done through the interdependence of proximity and distance. The study illustrates how good parenthood is made up of heterogeneous material and non-material entities such as patience, waiting, trust,

A. Sparrman (✉)
Department of Thematic Studies – Child Studies, Linköping University,
Linköping, Sweden
e-mail: anna.sparrman@liu.se

D. Cardell
Department of Sociology, Örebro University, Örebro, Sweden

A.-L. Lindgren
Department of Child and Youth Studies, Stockholm University, Stockholm,
Sweden

T. Samuelsson
School of Education and Communication, Jönköping University, Jönköping,
Sweden

© The Author(s) 2016
A. Sparrman et al. (eds.), *Doing Good Parenthood*, Palgrave Macmillan
Studies in Family and Intimate Life, DOI 10.1007/978-3-319-46774-0_10

113

wallets, mobile phones, age and the like; what is here called "the ontological choreography of (good) parenthood". The article draws on theories of doing family, making parents and family practice.

Keywords Togetherness · Doing parenthood · Ontological choreography of good parenthood · Childhood studies · Leisure

This chapter focuses on parenthood as being done in and through three child cultural establishments: the Swedish amusement park Liseberg (LB, Gothenburg), the Swedish theme park Astrid Lindgren's World (ALW, Vimmerby)[1] and the US-based children's museum Children's Museum of the Arts (CMA, New York).[2] Inspired by theoretical concepts like doing parents (e.g. Finch 2007; Gatrell 2005; Morgan 1996), making parents (e.g. Thompson 2005) and family practice (e.g. Finch 2007; Gatrell 2005; Morgan 1996), which were presented in the introduction to this book, we explore how good parenthood is being done in cultural practices.

Much of the emphasis in theories and research on the sociology of families has been on how the involved social actors take part in constructing family life (Gatrell 2005). In research on leisure activities, it is shown how leisure is constitutive of family life (Frønes 2009). Photographs displayed on walls taken during holidays and visits to zoos, for example, are important in creating family biographies. Increasingly, family visits to leisure activities are perceived as fundamental to constituting the rituals of not just any family, but a good family (Hallman and Benbow 2010). As families spend time doing fun things together in family-friendly places like zoos, quality family time is also performed (Hallman and Benbo 2010, 11). Bonnie C. Hallman and S. Mary P. Benbow (2010) even point out that American self-help literature suggests that getting away from home and doing things together makes it possible for families to (re)connect and (re)engage as families. Central to this discussion is the belief that visits to leisure establishments shape family togetherness, and that togetherness constitutes goodness (Hallman and Benbo 2010):

> Family leisure activities such as a trip to the zoo provide a context that links the practice of family-oriented leisure and the outcome of successful parenting, of being a "good parent", and the creation and sustaining of a positive, healthy, "successful" family life. (Hallman and Benbo 2010, 14)

Although togetherness through leisure activities is deemed to be constitutive of the good parent, Hallman and Benbow (2010) never define or unpack the concept. As described by the interviewed mothers and in the self-help literature, togetherness seems to be equated with time spent together, closeness and togetherness as cohesion, what we will here call "intensive togetherness". This is the case even though the same mothers describe zoo visits as children running around in the park while parents watch them from a distance. Given this unspecified connection between togetherness and goodness described in the literature, we want to explore how togetherness is constituted in practice through ethnographic visits to child cultural establishments. Our questions are: How and in what ways is togetherness enacted in cultural practices? And what features constitute it as good?

The Study

The analysis draws on research material from ethnographic walking-with and participant observations at three sites of child cultural establishments. Liseberg and ALW were visited together with ten families, while distanced participant observations were made at the Children's Museum of the Arts. The data was collected using cameras, video recordings, ethnographic field notes, interviewing and visual documentation (see also Cardell 2015; Lindgren et al. 2015; Samuelsson et al. 2015; Sparrman et al. 2015).

To capture what is going on in practice, the analytical tactic has been to break down the family concept into smaller components: children, parents, mothers and fathers. A practise-based approach to parenthood focuses on what, or who, does the doing. This means focusing on how (good) parenthood is brought into being, sustained and dissolved through different practices (cf. Mol 2002). The empirical examples have been chosen in order to illustrate how togetherness is enacted in and through practice to do good parenthood. As the literature emphasises intensive togetherness as cohesion, the two terms "proximity" and "distance" are used to explore it in practice.

Proximity and Distance: The Ontological Choreography of Good Parenthood

Material products for children like sleep guards, pushchairs, baby chairs and technological devices have long been important when planning the arrival of new-born babies. These are products that make parents, children and families, and shape notions of parenthood (Miller 1997; Sjöberg 2013; Thompson 2005). In these cases, the dynamic between the material and non-material is integral to the doing of parenthood. Charis Thompson (2005) uses the concept of "ontological choreography" to study reproductive technologies and the making of parents. This concept takes into account the balancing process of how things that are generally considered to be part of different ontological orders come together – that is, part of nature, part of the self, part of society. It is necessary for these elements to be coordinated in staged ways to proceed with the task at hand: producing children, parents, and whatever else is needed for their recognition as such (Thompson 2005, 8). To focus more on the connection between the material and non-material, our aim is to broaden the range of empirical data about parenthood. Our focus is on what we call the "ontological choreography of (good) parenthood".

Bounded Distance as Proximity

Child cultural establishments like theme parks and children's museums are created with children in mind. Families who decide to visit these places have thus decided to visit child-friendly activities together. Astrid Lindgren's World (ALW) and the Children's Museum of the Arts (CMA) have both accommodated their activities and functions to children's bodies. ALW's miniature houses, for example, are not accessible to adult body sizes (Fig. 10.1), and CMA's height-adjustable furniture is mainly adjustable to different child-sized bodies (Fig. 10.2). If parents are not prepared to bend down, double themselves up and crawl into the exhibited miniature houses at ALW (Fig. 10.1), or squeeze down onto height-adjustable child-flexible furniture at the CMA (Fig. 10.2), what can or do they do during visits to these places?

While children run in and out of the miniature houses at ALW (Fig. 10.1), parents can be seen standing around waiting and watching their children from a distance (Cardell 2015). Physically, children in these situations are closer to, and connect and interact with, other children inside the houses, rather than with their parents. At times, the waiting leads to parents beginning to occupy themselves in other ways. Some use their smartphones to take photos of their children. Photos are uploaded to be shared via social media in real time (see also Lindgren and Sparrman 2014). In these situations, parents connect with people outside the park, and share comments with them. Just like their children, they bond with

Fig. 10.1 Miniature houses at Astrid Lindgren's World, Kajsa Kavat. Picture from the visual documentation "Culture for and by Children"

Fig. 10.2 Adjustable furniture at CMA. Pictures from the visual documentation "Culture for and by children"

people beyond the family during the visit. Parents and children visit together and spend time in the same fenced geographical area. However, the miniature buildings position children and parents physically apart from one another, leading them to focus on activities involving different content.

A similar relation between children and parents arise when families visit CMA. While ALW is a large outdoor establishment $(130,000 \text{ m}^2)$, CMA occupies a limited, indoor space. The reason is at least twofold; firstly, financing and, secondly, because the museum primarily targets children. The interior design and furniture is therefore mainly fitted to children (Fig. 10.2). The museum offers neither a café nor a restaurant for visitors.

Even though the furniture is height adjustable at CMA, it does not easily fit adults. A lack of vacant chairs might also limit the possibilities for parents to sit down next to their child. Some parents stand and watch their child's activities over their shoulders. Yet, others have planned their visit before arrival. In these cases, parents read books, newspapers or smart tablets they have brought with them, and are firmly stationed on the movable bench in the exhibition hall (Fig. 10.3). These parents never have any intention of engaging with the museum's content. Instead they

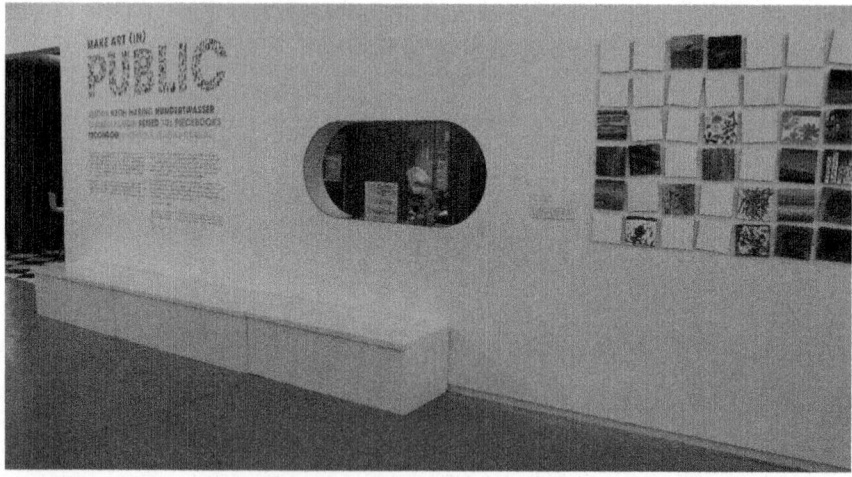

Fig. 10.3 Movable benches in the exhibition hall at CMA. Picture form the visual documentation "Culture for and by Children"

do what can be considered adult activities within a child-focused establishment.

Another observation from CMA was that it is rare to see nuclear families visiting together. The most common combination is child-adult or two adults, both with children. Without any further investigations one could ask: is this a result of the limited space?

So, while parents are seated in the exhibition hall, children participate in artistic activities in the creativity rooms. In these cases, children and parents have no physical or visual contact. The museum's limited space and the parents' central and stationary position in the exhibition hall make them easy to find. When children move to new activities or want to show off one of their creations, they seek out their parents. Parents are thus accessible to their children in this way. The proximity between the parent and child is made up of one stable and one mobile point, and a mutual understanding between the child and the parent that this is how the visit is carried out.

ALW and CMA's organisation of space and size choreograph the ways in which parenthood is being done. Space, body size and age intertwine in sustaining physical distance between the family members. At the same time, the material boundaries of the establishments (fences and walls) situate the families in the same time-space, outside their homes. Proximity and distance are not transferrable between the institutions as they are made up of different things in the different practices. For example, distance is created at ALW through large space, and at CMA through limited space, while proximity at ALW is created by being visible, staying around, waiting and moving when the children move, while at CMA for some it means being invisible but located at the same point all the time so that the child can find you. Even though the effect is similar for the child, waiting around also differs; waiting at ALW is seemingly unforeseen, while at CMA it is strategically planned in advance as part of the museum visit. Parenthood is choreographed through intertwinements of natural (body size), social (interaction with others), and material (furniture, buildings, boundaries) components (cf. Thompson 2005).

Mobile-Phone Proximity

Nine-year-old Tove is a big fan of the Nordic countries' largest amusement park, Liseberg (Cardell 2015). Her parents have mixed feelings about the park; nevertheless, they have given Tove full access to it by purchasing her an annual pass and accompanying her to the park on a weekly basis. These visits, however, are not carried out as ordinary nuclear family visits. The mother and father take turns and they talk about themselves in terms of a "support or service team" (Cardell 2015, 155–158). They are on standby in case Tove needs something while in the park. During the visits, the accompanying parent spends time at different places in the park, working, drinking coffee or strolling around, while Tove moves between and into the attractions on her own. The mobile and fluid nature of the visit is managed by connecting and communicating through mobile phones.[3]

The mobile phones set up an invisible relationship and connection across the large park area (1 km^2) between the attending parent and Tove. They are integrated material components, incorporating and choreographing the making of parenthood and childhood. The phones are fundamental to accomplishing this type of family visit to the amusement park. It is significant though that Tove and her parents fulfil their agreement of how to use the phones, to make the visits run smoothly. From a parental perspective, the phones stand out as control devices just as much as tools for creating proximity through standby. We do not know what would happen if Tove suddenly stopped using the phone. However, the parents are also controlled. Tove can call at any time for support and interrupt what they are doing; that is, the phones inflect on and limit the ways in which the parents spend their time in the park. While they allow Tove and the accompanying parent to engage in different activities in the park, the mobile phones open up opportunities for both distance and proximity in the parent-child interaction. This spatial and physical distance operates through mobile-phone proximity.

Thus, a material object is a central agent in the making and doing of parenthood (Morgan 1996; Thompson 2005). Being a good parent means allowing Tove to do what she enjoys the most while her parents do not need to ride on the attractions, but instead do what they want to do; for example, work. The phones enact family togetherness through proximity. From this, it follows that trust – trust in one another – becomes yet another strong immaterial bond between parent and child. Tove's and her parents' park visits are thus neither about reconnecting or reengaging as a family nor about having fun through intensive togetherness (Hallman and Benbo 2010). To some extent, the mobile phones even out the power relations between the child and the parent during these visits. Parenthood and childhood are choreographed by two mature, responsible and rational parties who simultaneously enact self-governing freedom and control through mobile phones (cf. Smith 2012; Thompson 2005).

Money and a Wallet as Proximity and Distance

Tony and Gill, the father and mother of the two boys Eric (age 5) and Jacob (age 7) visit ALW together as a family. As they walk around the park, the mother and boys walk closely together, followed at a short distance by Tony, the father. The closeness between the mother, Eric and Jacob makes Tony deliberately step back to create space for them. He even argues this is what the family expects of him. Now and then Tony talks on the phone, dealing with work matters. Suddenly, he happily exclaims to the researcher that he has sold a car (Cardell 2015). This, he adds, will finance the visit to ALW. The topic of money is central to Tony's fatherhood. He describes that he is drawn into the family activities when something needs to be paid for. Tony carries the wallet (Cardell 2015).

Observing the family from the outside, it seems that Tony and Gill have quite gender stereotypical parental positions: the father earns and provides money for the family, while the mother sees to the emotional care of the sons (Gatrell 2005). In this way, parenthood is made up of sets of components attached to either motherhood or fatherhood. The choreographing of Tony's parenthood is achieved by his relations to his phone, the labor market, the wallet with the money, the spatial distance, the mother, the children and gender stereotypes. Tony, Gill, Eric and Jacob have travelled to the park together, to spend time together; nevertheless, the distance between the family members makes Tony indirectly express minor concerns about marginalisation, even though he has a very clear and well-distinguished position in the family. He keeps the children's consumption to an acceptable level by providing and limiting access to money when asked for. Good fatherhood in this sense is done by both limiting and enabling consumption. The park plays a significant role in how Tony's fatherhood is being choreographed. Few parents see ALW as a straightforward commercial arena, they look upon it rather as good child culture (Cardell 2015). This is where Tony's wallet comes in. He makes sure the cultural content and market consumption are balanced by making decisions about what can and cannot be purchased. Tony does not express general discontent with his fatherhood, but his ambivalence illustrates that doing good parenthood is not the same for a father and a mother. The significant factors for Tony to be a good father at ALW are money, his wallet, and the time he has set aside to visit ALW with his family (Cardell 2015).

CONCLUDING DISCUSSION

This chapter has explored how family togetherness and good parenthood relate to one another when conducting family visits to child cultural establishments such as children's museums, theme parks and amusement parks. The analyses challenge earlier assumptions that intensive family togetherness – such as closeness, spending time together and cohesion – are the only ways of constituting good parenthood (Hallman and Benbo 2010).

The examples show that families do visit child-oriented cultural establishments together. Our practice-based approach demonstrates, however, that togetherness is performed by interlinking proximity and distance in multiple ways across institutional practices and across families. Parents and children continuously move in and out of being physically close, or distant from one another. Stability is established in some families through (in)visible parents watching and waiting around for their children, while other families move around and connect via mobile phones. Material as well as non-material, natural as well as cultural, and abstract as well as physical entities are all part of how parenthood is being done during these visits. Such varied components as waiting around, self-entertainment, newspapers, trust, mobile phones, wallets, furniture, labour, age, body size, independence and benevolent children all make up parenthood. Social interactions, materiality, technologies, emotions and aspects of nature are all equivalently intertwined and productive components in the making. All families manage and organise their visits through the interdependent parameters of distance and proximity. This, we argue, is done to manage togetherness. Strategies for handling this back-and-forth movement, as pointed out, differ between places, families and situations. Taking all these aspects into consideration leads to what we call "the ontological choreography of (good) parenthood" (cf. Thompson 2005). So, if family visits to child-oriented cultural establishments are heterogeneous and conducted through complex and multiple relations between proximity and distance, and not solely through physical togetherness, is it then possible to talk about doing good parenthood through togetherness?

The analyses clearly reveal that good parenthood cannot be understood through one concept or action. When we unpack togetherness and break down the family into fathers, mothers, children and other crucial material and non-material entities, it becomes obvious that the good is choreographed through the dynamic processes situated within each individual family. To be a good parent involves setting aside time to do child-focused activities, having the patience to wait around, assist, and engage. What is unexpected, however, is that to be a good parent in these practices also implies managing one's own lack of interest and dissatisfactions. While "soccer-mums" (Williams and Crumplin 2010, 42) are described as putting their children's priorities first, the culture parent does well both for the child and her/himself. The multiple ways in which good parenthood is choreographed through the joint family visit tell us that intensive togetherness is not the only way of conducting good parenthood. It can also be done, as the analyses in this chapter show, by trying to harmonise proximity and distance to the satisfaction of all the involved family members. So, maybe, doing well enough for everyone is the doing of good parenthood.

NOTES

1. Astrid Lindgren wrote the famous children's book *Pippi Longstocking*, among many others.
2. Funded by the Swedish Research Council Hum-Sam, Dnr 2009–2384. *Culture for and by children.*
3. When Tove was younger, they used walkie-talkies (Cardell 2015).

REFERENCES

Cardell, D. 2015. *Family theme parks, happiness and children's consumption: From roller-coaster to Pippi Longstocking*, Ph.D. thesis, Department of Thematic Studies – Child Studies. Linköping: Linköping University.

Finch, J. 2007. "Displaying families." *Sociology* 41(1): 65–81.

Frønes, I. 2009. "Childhood: Leisure, culture and peers." In *Palgrave handbook of childhood studies*, edited by J. Qvortrup, W. Corsaro, and M.-S. Honig, 273–286. Basingstoke: Palgrave Macmillan.

Gatrell, C. 2005. *Hard labour: The sociology of parenthood*. Maidenhead: Open University Press.

Hallman, B.C., and M.P. Benbo. 2010. "'Seeing if you can catch the one picture that just makes it': Placing family life through family zoo photography."

In *Family geographies: The spatiality of families and family life*, edited by B.C. Hallman, 10–30. Oxford: Oxford University Press.

Lindgren, A.-L., and A. Sparrman. 2014. "Blogging family-like relations when visiting theme and amusement parks: The use of children in display online." *Culture Unbound* 6: 997–1013.

Lindgren, A.-L., A. Sparrman, T. Samuelsson and D. Cardell. 2015. "Enacting (real) fiction: Materializing childhoods in a theme park." *Childhood* 22(2): 171–186.

Miller, D. 1997. "How infants grow mothers in North London." *Theory, Culture, & Society* 14(4): 67–88.

Mol, A. 2002. *The body multiple: Ontology in medical practice.* Durham: Duke University Press.

Morgan, D.H.J. 1996. *Family connections.* Cambridge: Polity Press.

Samuelsson, T., A. Sparrman, D. Cardell and A.-L Lindgren. 2015. "The active, competent child, capable of autonomous action: An inherent quality or the outcome of a research process?" *AnthropoChildren* 5 [Online].

Sjöberg, J. 2013. *I marknadens öga: Barn och visuell konsumtion.* [In the eye of the market: Children and visual consumption], Ph.D. thesis, Department of Thematic Studies – Child Studies. Linköping: Linköping University.

Smith, K. 2012. "Producing governable subjects: Images of childhood old and new." *Childhood* 19(24): 24–37.

Sparrman, A., T. Samuelsson, A-L Lindgren, and D. Cardell. 2015. "The ontological practices of child culture." *Childhood* 23(2): 255–271.

Thompson, C. 2005. *Making parents: The ontological choreography of reproductive technologies.* Cambridge, MA: The MIT Press.

Williams, D., and W. Crumplin. 2010. "The impact of travel on families with youth competitive athletes." In *Family geographies: The spatiality of families and family life*, edited by B.C. Hallman, 31–50. Oxford: Oxford University Press.

Anna Sparrman, Ph.D., is a professor at the Department of Thematic Studies – Child Studies, Linköping University, Sweden. Her general research interests concern norms and values of children and childhood by combining visual culture, child consumption, child culture and child sexuality. She was research leader of the research project "Culture for and by Children" and has recently published *The ontological practice of child culture* together with her collaborators. Sparrman has a special interest in ethnography and visual research methods.

David Cardell, Ph.D., is a researcher and lecturer in sociology at Örebro University, Sweden. He is particularly interested in happiness, childhood and capitalism. Cardell has previously conducted interdisciplinary research on commercial youth sport and theme parks, focusing on children, family practices and organisation. He holds research degrees in sports and child studies, from the universities of Örebro and Linköping.

Anne-Li Lindgren, Ph.D., is Professor of Child and Youth Studies at Stockholm University, Sweden, where she is director of the Early Childhood Education section. She is also a member of the scientific committee at the Agency for Swedish Cultural Policy Analysis. Her current research focuses on childhood visualisations and child cultures in early childhood education from historical and contemporary perspectives.

Tobias Samuelsson, Ph.D., is Associate Professor in Sociology at the School of Education and Communication, Jönköping University, Sweden. His area of research covers ethnographic studies of family life and children's everyday lives, with a particular focus on child culture and children's work. His research focuses on children and their interplay with surrounding social, cultural and material frames.

CHAPTER 11

Parenthood and We-ness in Everyday Life: Parenting Together Apart

Allan Westerling

Abstract This chapter explores narratives of sharing parental responsibility in everyday life among parents who do not live together. It is a social-psychological analysis of qualitative interview data focusing on family relations and social networks in everyday life in Denmark. The interview data stem from a large research project on the consequences of individualisation for social networks and family life. One of the dilemmas of post-divorce parenting comprises sharing parental responsibility while simultaneously separating from the other parent. Applying a case-based analysis, two interpretative frameworks of good parenthood is identified: devotion and symmetry. Moreover, it is discussed how these frameworks intersect with the conflict narrative of divorce. To further explore the meaning of good post-divorce parenting, a concept of *we-ness* is introduced in the context of divorce. The chapter concludes by arguing that post-divorce parenthood can be understood as reinventing the family (Beck-Gernsheim 2002) and re-constituting we-ness in novel ways.

Keywords Post divorce parenting · We-ness · Conflict · Narrative approach · Recognition · Sociological imagination · Social psychology

A. Westerling (✉)
Center for Childhood, Youth & Family Life Research, Department of People & Technology, Roskilde University, Roskilde, Denmark
e-mail: allanw@ruc.dk

© The Author(s) 2016   127
A. Sparrman et al. (eds.), *Doing Good Parenthood*, Palgrave Macmillan Studies in Family and Intimate Life, DOI 10.1007/978-3-319-46774-0_11

Often seen as the end of a family and usually associated with conflict, divorce entails new forms of households and cohabitation. Divorce nonetheless rarely means the end of parenting for any of the adults involved; on the contrary, even stronger demands are placed on the parents to cooperate about the diverse aspects of parenthood (Ottosen 1997). Deciding who the child or children should stay with – and when – is one issue but cooperating about schoolwork, leisure activities, consumption, relationships to other kin and grandparents also poses challenges for divorced parents. How can post-divorce parenthood be done? How is parenting divided and distributed after a break up? What is good parenthood in this situation?

Based on the backdrop that parenting must be done together, in some form of collaboration, while being apart, these broad questions have to be addressed in the family life that emerges after divorce. This leads to at least one central dilemma: How is it possible to do good parenthood when a central feature of parenting – togetherness – is absent? I explore post-divorce parenthood by analysing togetherness in everyday life. The analysis is based on data drawn from a single interview case comprising narratives on the difficulties post-divorce parenting presents. I analyse these troubles (Mills 1959) and challenges as a means to explore good parenthood.

THE STUDY

The qualitative interview data are from a longitudinal research project and panel study on Family Life and Cohabitation in the Modern Welfare State (FAMOSTAT) (Dencik et al. 2003, 2008; Westerling 2008, 2010, 2015), originally funded by the Danish National Research Council. The first wave of data was collected in 2003 and 2004 (n = 983) and the second in 2014 (n = 431). Based on a preliminary analysis of the 2003 questionnaire responses, a strategic subsample of individuals 35–36 years of age (n = 15) was selected to participate in semi-structured, face-to-face interviews in 2003 and 2004 lasting 100–120 minutes.

The interviews focused on the participants' social networks and relationships in everyday life. For the questionnaire, participants are called respondents but were approached as informants for the qualitative interview (Kvale and Brinkmann 2009; Spradley 1979). Informants are assumed to be knowledgeable experts about their everyday life, the interviewer acting as a facilitator to support informants with the reflexive resources to articulate the experiences of everyday life. In practice, this means providing informants with opportunities to describe, elaborate and evaluate the events and experiences of everyday life. This means that the interviews were about narrating everyday life in the interview situation. The interviews were transcribed and the informants' names and any distinguishing characteristics changed to preserve the anonymity of informants. This article presents an in-depth analysis of one interview from 2004. Out of the 15 interviews, 8 were with adults, 4 of whom were women, living a post-divorce family life.

The analysis focuses on the configurations of communality and individuality in everyday family life as narrated and negotiated in the qualitative interviews. The analysis identifies interpretative frameworks of everyday life (van den Berg et al. 2003), and the positions that can be taken up and negotiated within these frameworks (Davies and Harré 1990; Harré and Moghaddam 2003; Søndergaard 2000). Approaching the analysis in this way makes it possible to include the interaction between the interviewer and the informant but does not limit its claim on the interview interaction alone. As such, the analysis departs from the narrative co-constructions in the interview setting.

THEORY AND ANALYTICAL FOCUS

Post-divorce parenting can be understood as one of the modern ways of doing parenthood that transgresses conventional categories in family studies (see the introductory chapter Beck-Gernsheim 2002; Roseneil and Budgeon 2004) Post-divorce parenting comprises processes concerning coordination, conflict and collaboration across households, often involving more than just two parents as step-parents and new partners also play a vital part in post-divorce family life. Thomas Johansson and Margareta Bäck-Wiklund (2003) suggest conceptualising some of the new ways of doing family as *network families*. The network family is a conceptual prism that allows the study of family life in terms of relationships rather than as pre-conceptualised categories. In keeping with this line of thinking, studying post-divorce parenthood involves looking at how collaboration, togetherness and we-ness are constituted and distributed across the social networks of everyday family life.

I argue (Westerling 2008) that the social mode, rather than the patterns of cohabitation or household structure, should be studied if the aim is to understand the novelty of family life. This approach means taking a social psychological perspective as it implies a conceptualisation of the relationship between the individual and social aspects as one of mutual interdependence and interchange (Asplund 1983; Dencik 2005; Simmel 1908).

The subsequent analysis is based on an interview I conducted with Gitte, 35, who has been divorced from George, 36, for a little over 4 years. They live in the same town and have two girls, Fiona, 8, and Hannah, 10, who live with Gitte for 9 days and then George for 5. This agreement was made under supervision and counselling from the regional state authority dealing primarily with issues concerning family law.

Gitte is forthcoming, rapidly feeling comfortable enough during the interview to share intimate details. She vividly describes her divorce, current love life (she is romantically involved with Greg) and the conflicts she has with her ex-husband. At the start of the interview, Gitte explains that she has multiple sclerosis, which works as a key constituent in many (but not all) of the narratives she and I co-construct (Gubrium and Holstein 2012) during the interview. Her diagnosis and medical history are not explicitly articulated as we talk, though they are at times implicitly inferred, absent or inactive.

INTERPRETATIVE FRAMEWORKS OF PARENTHOOD

Gitte's accounts of post-divorce family life are filled with tension and conflict; George is described as being unable to curb his animosity towards her, which Gitte says affects their ability to cooperate about the children. She describes how George overemphasises his owns feelings of hurt and privation when it comes to the children and states, "This is not about what he feels. It's about the children and nothing but the children. He needs to hide his own hurt feelings, really, and then give the children a better life, right. That's what it's all about for me."

Gitte's account presents George as performing bad parenting. He is unable to set his own feelings aside and focus on the children. According to Gitte, he quite literally needs to suppress his feelings of hurt and rejection to keep them outside of the relationship. Gitte evaluates: George should do this and invest his emotional energy in his relationship with his daughters. The interpretative framework of good parenthood is about sacrifice, which entails that good parents must give up what they want for the sake of the children. To be a good parent includes focusing on the needs of the children, ignoring – or at least postponing – the needs of one self. Gitte elaborates.

Gitte: Well, I would've liked to have the children with me for Christmas. But that's just the way it is when you're divorced. I just have to wish the kids a merry Christmas and say, "You know – at your grandma's [George's mother] – it's really nice, right...gold plates and everything. We'll just have something another day at home, okay?!"

And I know they've a great Christmas at grandma's. And I'm not supposed to say

"Oh, what about me? I have to be all alone with Greg while you have a great time at grandma's." No, that's just the way it is...

George can't do that. I mean [makes her voice deeper] "Oh no, daddy doesn't get to set off the real fancy fireworks with you guys on New Year's Eve." [changes back to her own voice] Right, but you had them at Christmas! Next year it's the other way around.

They feel so bad for daddy because he didn't really buy fireworks because we weren't there. He shouldn't let the children know about this. He should tell them that he had the greatest New Year's and that they will have a great New Year next year and the years after that. The children shouldn't have to worry – not the way adults worry. That's my opinion!

In this narrative, Gitte invokes the ideal of devoted parents who ignore themselves to focus on the children's needs. The narrative also unfolds, however, in front of the backdrop of yet another ideal: the equal distribution of time. In Gitte's case, this ideal is formalised based on the regional state authority's division of Fiona's and Hannah's days between Gitte and George. Sharing time with children is a central topic of concern in post-divorce parenthood, but this is also the case for married or cohabiting parents when it comes to sharing care, which should be done equally or at least equitably (Westerling 2008). The overarching ideal is balanced reciprocity. When Gitte talks about the distribution of time with the children, her implicit claim is that the parents' right to time with their children must be equally distributed.

Based on this analysis, it is possible to identify two different interpretative frameworks of good parenthood. On the one hand, good parenthood means putting the children first and being devoted. This ideal of good parenthood, articulated in Gitte's narrative, involves self-sacrifice and being attentive to the needs of others, in the case her children. This ideal can also be interpreted as an expression of love, where you become yourself *with* another person. It is a fusion of one's identity and agenda with the agenda and needs of the object of love (Honneth 1996).

On the other hand, good post-divorce parenthood revolves around a symmetrical distribution of time. This is articulated as a source of conflict when George is unable to accept the agreed distribution of parental time with the children. This ideal can be interpreted as an expression of respect. To respect someone means to recognise their wishes, perspectives and rights as valid, regardless of one's own position. In Gitte's narrative of parental cooperation, her rights are sanctioned and supported by the formalisation of their children's visitation agreement (alternating between nine days with Gitte and five days with George) but challenged by George.

Consequently, a conflict can be identified between these two interpretative frameworks of good parenthood. The conflict dynamic lies between disregarding oneself (for the sake of the children) and asserting oneself and one's rights (to be with and to care for the children), for instance, between letting go and holding on. These frameworks of good parenthood are not merely abstract ideals. They become meaningful and active in the concrete terrain of everyday family life. In this sense, these frameworks of good parenthood intersect with the challenges and tensions of family life, which the following section demonstrates. In Gitte's case, the conflict elements of good parenthood intersect with the plot of the divorce narrative.

Parenthood in Conflict Territory

Gitte's account of the divorce is structured by a description of her (failed) struggles for recognition from George. This narrative describes how she gained greater personal integrity and dignity by excluding George from her life. She emphasises this by dismissing George as someone with the ability to contribute to her happiness and well-being, recounting an episode that occurred one evening when suffered an attack of multiple sclerosis prior to diagnosis:

> Gitte: [T]hat night, when I had the attack, when I lost my hearing and my vision blurred and I fainted and stuff, you know, and I asked him to take me to the hospital – and this was right after I was diagnosed as a hypochondriac – he simply refused to take me to the hospital. I just had to pull myself together, right? And someone like that is someone I can't live with. I need to know that the people around me are people I can trust, you know. And that they'll help me and that they believe what I say, right.

This account is structured around a plot involving the fight for recognition. George is in a position where he denies Gitte recognition. When he refuses to take her to the hospital, he fails to recognise her suffering and, as such, does not show respect for or validate Gitte's interpretation of herself. He simply does not recognise Gitte's integrity. Elsewhere during the interview, Gitte elaborates on her feelings of abandonment. She was left alone. In this account, George is not there for her when she needs him to be. In this way, the plot that structures Gitte's narrative of her divorce from George positions him as someone who neither meets the ideals of symmetry or devotion. As a result, the narrative of parenting intersects with the narrative of divorce. While they are not identical, the plotlines mirror one another in the sense that they also seem to amplify the conflict of cooperation.

The ideal of devotion is present when Gitte invokes blame, accusing George of not putting his own feelings aside for the sake of the children and when she narrates the break up, attributing it (partly) to George's failure to be there for her. Similarly, the ideal of symmetry is present when Gitte narrates how George was unable to respect her integrity during their marriage and when she describes his opposition to the agreed-upon division of sharing their time with their children in their post-divorce family life. Thus, the ideal of respect and symmetry seems to contradict the ideal of devotion and love. This contradiction is interconnected with the conflict of divorce. Gitte's rejection of we-ness with George as her partner intersects the absence of we-ness between Gitte and George as parents.

CONCLUDING DISCUSSION

Based on these analyses and discussions, I argue that the contradictions between symmetry and devotion are a potential conflict in parenthood as such. However, since parenting together mediates we-ness, there is also the potential for conflict resolution. While the framework of good parenthood as devotion brings the needs of children to centre stage, it also potentially mediates alignment between the parents. The parents are both secondary vis-á-vis their children. In other words, they share a position as dedicated and oriented towards their children's perspective and agenda, which could act as a foundation for we-ness. Similarly, the framework of good parenthood as symmetry entails equality or alignment in the parents' involvement with their children. As such, it implies likeness or sameness between the parents in relation to the children and could also support the development of we-ness.

In Gitte's case, none of these frameworks of good parenthood provides ample guidelines for we-ness in the everyday practices and negotiations of post-divorce parenthood. As shown, this is partially owed to the experience that divorce does not provide fertile soil for developing we-ness. I would also argue, however, that an equally important part of the reason Gitte's trouble in articulating we-ness in the narratives of parental cooperation lies in the unavailability of cultural resources. The interpretative frameworks of good parenthood available to Gitte do not enable her to navigate between doing together and being apart.

Gitte's narrative illustrates how post-divorce parenting means parenting together but apart. In this sense, parenting is articulated as a communal activity, something that parents do together, while the very feature of divorce is the opposite: separation from one's partner. In this light, Gitte's story represents the trouble of reinterpreting, and perhaps *reinventing* (Beck-Gernsheim 2002), the communal features of parenting. The problem that this reflects does not involve Gitte or George's personal incapability or imperfections but rather the lack of *sociological imagination* (Mills 1959) or perhaps cultural creativity in doing good post-divorce parenting. As a result, this means that being divorced parents means doing we-ness apart; it means being a network family rather than a nuclear family, thus requiring the rearticulation of good parenthood as separate parents who work together.

Consequently, Gitte's troubles reflect larger cultural issues, her everyday narratives of her struggle bearing witness to the gradual changes in good parenthood slowly but surely being worked out by parents in modern everyday life.

References

Asplund, J. 1983. *Tid, rum, individ och kollektiv* [Time, space, indvidual and community]. Stockholm: Liber Förlag.

Beck-Gernsheim, E. 2002. *Reinventing the family: In search of new lifestyles.* Cambridge and Oxford: Polity Press and Blackwell Publishers.

Davies, B., and R. Harré. 1990. "Positioning: The discursive production of selves." *Journal for the Theory of Social Behavior* 20(1): 43–63.

Dencik, L. 2005. *Mennesket i postmoderniseringen – om barndom, familie og identiteter i opbrud* [The human being during postmodernisation – on childhood, family and rupturing identities]. Værløse: Billesø & Baltzer.

Dencik, L., A Westerling, A. Stanek, and K. Marosi. 2003. *IFUSOFF–et instrument for undersøgelse af socialt fællesskab og familieliv [SONEFAL – an instrument for the study of comunality and family life]*. Roskilde: Center for Barndoms-& Familieforskning, Roskilde Universitetscenter.

Dencik, L., P.S. Jørgensen, and D. Sommer. 2008. *Familie og børn i en opbrudstid.* Copenhagen: Hans Reitzels Forlag.

Gubrium, J.F., and J.A. Holstein. 2012. "Narrative practice and the transformation of interview subjectivity." In *The SAGE handbook of interview research: The complexity of the craft*, edited by J.F. Gubrium, J.A. Holstein, A.B. Marvasti, and K.D. McKinney, 27–44. Los Angeles: Sage Publications.

Harré, R., and F.M. Moghaddam. 2003. *The self and others: Positioning individuals and groups in personal, political, and cultural contexts.* Westport: Praager Publishers.

Honneth, A. 1996. *The struggle for recognition: The moral grammar of social conflicts.* Cambridge: MIT Press.

Johansson, T., and M. Bäck-Wiklund, eds. 2003. *Nätverksfamiljen [The network family].* Stockholm: Natur och kultur.

Kvale, S., and S. Brinkmann. 2009. *Interviews: Learning the craft of qualitative research interviewing.* Los Angeles: Sage Publications.

Mills, C.W. 1959. *The social imagination.* New York: Oxford University Press.

Ottosen, M.H. 1997. *Børn i sammenbragte familier: Et studie af forældreskab som social konstruktion* [Children in reconstituted families. A study of parenthood as a social constrcution]. Copenhagen: Danish National Centre for Social Research.

Roseneil, S., and S. Budgeon. 2004. "Cultures of intimacy and care beyond 'the family': Personal life and social change in the early 21st century." *Current Sociology* 52(2): 135–159.

Simmel, G. 1908. *Soziologie: Untersuchungen über die formen der vergesellschaftung* [Sociology. investigatng the modes of societilization]. Leipzig: Duncker und Humblot.

Søndergaard, D.M. 2000. "Destabiliserende diskursanalyse" [Destablising discourse analysis]. In *Kjønn og fortolkende metode* [Gender and interpretive method], edited by Hanne Haavind, 60–104. Oslo: Gyldendal Akademisk.

Spradley, J.P. 1979. *The ethnographic interview.* Belmont: Wadsworth Group – Thomson Learning.

van den Berg, H., M. Wetherell, and H. Houtkoop-Steenstra. 2003. *Analyzing race talk: Multidisciplinary perspectives on the research interview.* Cambridge: Cambridge University Press.

Westerling, A. 2008. *Individualisering, familie og fællesskab: En socialpsykologisk analyse af hverdagslivets sociale netværk i en refleksiv modernitet* [Individualisation, family and communality. A social psychological analysis of the social networks of everyday life in a reflexive modernity]. PhD thesis, Department of Psychology and Educational Studies. Roskilde: Roskilde University.

Westerling, A. 2010. "Everyday family life: Investigating the individual/social in a radicalized modernity." In *Sustaining everyday life conference*, edited by K. Karlsson and K. Ellergård, 137–150. Linköping: Linköping University Electronic Press.

Westerling, A. 2015. "Reflexive fatherhood in everyday life: The case of Denmark." *Families, Relationships and Societies* 4(2): 209–223.

Allan Westerling, Ph.D., is Associate Professor at the Department of People & Technology, Roskilde University, Denmark. He is a member and co-founder of the Centre for Childhood, Youth and Family Life Research in this department. He is a social psychologist working across the fields of psychology and sociology. His area of research covers fatherhood, parenthood and family life. Particular interests include the institutionalisation of care under the Welfare State, and the consequences of individualisation for family life.

CHAPTER 12

Doing Good Parenthood: Reflexivity, Practices, and Relationships

Esther Dermott

Abstract In light of the findings detailed in the empirical chapters, the concluding chapter returns to the questions of what constitutes good parenthood and who defines the concept. It highlights the consequences of combining a family studies and childhood studies approach, and reflects on the contrast between Denmark and Sweden, and the UK. It offers some thoughts on how these research findings can be used to progress thinking about good parenthood and argues for the merit of placing parent-child relationships centre stage.

Keywords Bad · Display · Good · Normative · Parenthood · Parent-child relationship

Good parenthood is viewed as a necessity yet achieving it is elusive. Not least because there is a lack of agreement over what good parenthood should try to achieve and there are different parties involved in negotiating and delivering good parenthood.

The description of a new *intensive* parenthood in the 1990s suggested that the role of parents had undergone a steep change in terms of significantly

E. Dermott (✉)
School of Sociology, Politics and International Studies, University of Bristol, Bristol, UK
e-mail: Esther.Dermott@bristol.ac.uk

© The Author(s) 2016
A. Sparrman et al. (eds.), *Doing Good Parenthood*, Palgrave Macmillan
Studies in Family and Intimate Life, DOI 10.1007/978-3-319-46774-0_12

greater interest in how parenting should be done. This was, in turn, associated with increased surveillance over parents and discussion over how society as a whole should contribute to good parenthood. A key concern, perhaps especially within the disciplines of education, psychology, and policy, has been a desire to determine causal relationships between parental practices and outcomes for children. Yet decades of debate have produced little consensus over the objective of good parenthood; perhaps only in relation to ensuring that children are both taken seriously as independent social actors and supported to become successful adult citizens. These tend to include some combination of supporting relative independence; developing social skills; providing physical and emotional care; facilitating enjoyment/play; and promoting appropriate educational engagement. Perhaps, unsurprisingly then, how to measure good parenthood and its impact remains unclear. The chapters in this collection make an important contribution by shedding light on what parents and children feel are the priorities in doing good parenthood in terms both of practices and ideals. In doing so, these chapters also highlight the particular temporal, social and geographical contexts in which the doing of good parenthood is conducted.

There are a number of social actors involved in determining good parenthood. We expect parents to love and care for their children but often assume that they act as a single unit rather than as individuals who may be differently positioned because of the status they hold as biological or social parents, partners and ex-partners, or as mothers and fathers. Parents are also not the only actors involved. It is a requirement of the state to intervene in the lives of individual children whose parents have fallen below a certain standard of behaviour or, as illustrated in a number of these chapters, when legal practices such as adoption need to be managed. Government policies have also become important in setting out specific activities as markers of good parenthood and making general statements that reflect normative expectations. In these circumstances, parents must in some ways negotiate their own practices as a response to cultural prescriptions. Moving away from a view of parenthood that is solely about the activities of parents that are done *to* or *for* children necessarily encompasses a view of children as more active agents and, importantly, the interdependence of parents and children. The chapters here show how, on a micro level, the negotiation of good parenthood includes a wide range of social actors and how competing views, agendas and power relationships are played out. Significantly, the book as whole highlights the importance for family studies of not just taking children's voices seriously, but the value of engaging with child studies in order to see parenthood as intentionally relational.

The editors, in their introduction, state that their aim is to look at the relationship between ideals and practices of parenthood. This concluding chapter returns to some of the initial questions they posed as well as engaging with the findings detailed in the empirical chapters in terms of what constitutes good parenthood and who defines the concept. In addition, it offers some thoughts on how these research findings can be used to further unpack, and hopefully progress, thinking about doing good parenthood. The current status given to bad parenthood as a source of social problems, indeed a public health issue as well as the potential panacea for social problems, means that parenthood is both a weighty and contentious issue. This chapter takes up the theme of parent-child relationships and argues for the value of placing this centre stage.

Defining Doing Good Parenthood

In adopting the term *doing good parenthood* rather than doing good parenting the editors of this collection aim to highlight the existence of underlying culturally predefined ideas of *good* as captured through observable parenting practices: to illustrate how aspects of the normative emerge or are evident through everyday activities. My sense is that there are two main themes in how doing good parenthood is defined in these empirical accounts. First, the confirmation of a commitment to reflexive practice has a central position. Second, and notwithstanding this reflexivity, there do exist specific practices that are culturally and socially accepted as good. These two elements might seem to be in tension with each other as the first seems to be about fluidity and agency and the second continuity and constraint. However, the editors' and authors' framing of doing good parenthood as based on a strong parent-child relationship makes both elements possible.

Reflexivity

Thinking about the impact of different parental actions emerges as a key component to how many parents in the previous chapters talk about and display good parenthood. Perhaps the clearest example is in Judith Lind's analysis of how parents interact by posting queries and comments on a popular online Swedish parenting discussion board. Lind highlights how parents communicate in ways that are either accepted by other parents as good parenting or are criticised as unacceptable; even in some cases falling so far outside the remit of good parenting as to be labelled trolling. It is not the case that individual actions by parents simply determine the response they receive online, in fact, it is recognised that there exist a diversity of viewpoints and behaviours, and that different choices can be made in good faith. Rather, what is essential is to adopt a considered tone which, through choice of words and phrases, indicates that parents are willing to think about alternatives, are not overly hasty in making decisions, and do not simply resort to conclusions based on their own predilections rather than referencing the needs of their child. The requirement for good parenthood to be reflexive is in sync with Gidden's *project of the self* (1998), which sees critical reflexivity as central to the process of transforming intimate relations in late modernity, with a shift towards more equal, democratic and reciprocal personal relationships. The centrality of reflexivity could therefore be viewed as an inherently positive move, particularly for reorienting the power dynamics between parents and children and providing a counter to parental determinism. This move would also be consistent with developments within child studies over recent decades. There is evidence in the chapters in this collection that recognising, and engaging with, the desires and opinions of children – taking children seriously as social actors – is indeed seen as a key component to doing good, reflexive parenthood.

There is a strong sense from the chapters that the requirement to both engage reflexive thinking about good parenthood and display it are frequently mandated by external agencies including in the Danish and Swedish context welfare state institutions. That is, reflexivity is not necessarily a mark of the individualisation of parenthood as Anthony Giddens' (1998) account would suggest. Most notably in the chapters by Cecilia Lindgren and Pernille Juhl on adoption agencies and child protection services respectively, there is evidence of how parents are expected to reflect on and display their practices in order to achieve recognition that they are doing good parenthood. This could be used as an argument for reflexivity not only being a component of good *parenting* (if this is taken to be individual practices) but of good *parenthood* which, as outlined by the editors in their introduction, also encompasses cultural ideals. It also highlights how the requirement to be reflexive depends on social location. Those with less social power either because of how they are defined as parents or because their class or ethnicity places them outside the dominant mode of parenting are required to reaffirm their reflexive engagement with the project of good parenthood to a greater degree. This is illustrated in the accounts produced by Disa Bergnehr and Maria Ørskov Akselvoll of school teachers' expectations about how parents should communicate. This argument fits with Janet Finch's concept of *displaying families* (2007): she argues that everyday family practices need to be recognised by others in order to count and that the need for display becomes more acute the more different family relationships are from conventional ideas of family.

As noted above, reflexivity seems to imply that, at least from the perspective of parents, there should be serious consideration of the impact of their actions for children with the *best interests of the child* coming to the fore, alongside a broad ongoing dialogue with children about the ideals and practices involved in good parenthood. Indeed, it is interesting to note how a consideration of a child's well-being has become institutionalised. In the UK context, for example in legal cases that involve children such as the organisation of care arrangement post-divorce or whether parental religious views should be allowed to determine the kind of medical care a child receives, it is the *best interests of the child* that is the principle against which any course of action must be judged. In this context, the expression of an alternative view that is acknowledged in Anna Malmquist, Anna Polski, and Karin Zetterqvist Nelson's chapter on the rationale for using anonymous sperm donors by lesbian couples is perhaps surprising. Most of the mothers interviewed emphasised the positive value of anonymous sperm donation for children by confirming the status of their family unit and the role of both mothers. Yet, some mothers said that their preference was "selfish" and had more to do with their own desires than an assessment of what was best for their child. The reason why this is a surprising comment is that, in adopting a version of good parenthood in which the views and values of children need to be taken seriously, it becomes more difficult for parents to admit that an action is for selfish reasons.

Finally, there is, I think, a strong caveat to the claim that reflexivity alone should be labelled as the primary marker of good parenthood. The requirement to display that one is thinking about the impact of parental behaviours and engaging with cultural expectations around parenthood may stop short of genuine reflexivity as defined as a willingness to evaluate and challenge one's own taken-for-granted position and ways of being. What is evident from interviews with parents that are quoted in this edited collection is that it is very important to present to relevant others that a rationale for particular behaviours and attitudes exists. This version of reflexivity involves a requirement to *display* (cf. Finch 2007) that parenting is being thought about, thus signifying that parenthood is a serious undertaking that requires careful consideration. However, this may involve finding a plausible post-hoc rationalisation of decision making rather than suggesting a genuine open reflection about possible courses of action.

PARENTING PRACTICES

While reflexivity is important, there is also a clear sense from the chapters that parenthood is not determined only by recourse to internal dialogue or conversations. The research in this collection reflects a number of characteristics and attributes of children that parents are expected to support to a greater or lesser degree: creativity; academic achievement; sporting acumen; sociability. While these ideals themselves exist in a particular historical and culturally specific moment, they do offer societal reference points for behaviour. In some cases, it is even stronger than this, in that particular tropes seemingly *must* be referenced in order for a position to be accepted as valid. To refer again to Lind's chapter on how parents post and respond to online discussion boards, it is clear that, while there is indeed a requirement to show reflexivity, there is also a view that sexual relationships are an individual right of teenagers so that parents should only intervene if there is a health risk or other serious concern that must be well justified. What good parenthood is trying to achieve becomes especially visible when there are conflicting perspectives. In Dil Bach's analysis of how educational practices are debated in Denmark and Singapore, what emerges is the relative importance of educational attainment and social interactions in different national contexts.

In the UK, the examples of parent-child activities most frequently held up as exemplars of good parenthood are education related, such as reading to children, using a wide vocabulary and helping with homework; categorised by Frank Field MP (2010) as the "home learning environment". Esther Dermott and Marco Pomati (2016) have argued that in the UK, a narrow set of practices that are mainly education focused and which have attained status as markers of good parenthood have largely been adopted by parents, suggesting something of a consensus; in line with the argument that contemporary good parenting has been characterised as an "affiliation to a certain way of raising a child" (Faircloth and Lee 2010, 1.2). From a UK perspective in which much of the policy discussion has centred on developing a model of good parenthood that will result in the development of future good citizens and has placed educational attainment high up its list of priorities, it is interesting to observe that a number of chapters in this collection also discuss the role of education. Bach on the framing of "ambitious parents" in educational settings; Akselvoll on online parent-school interactions; and Disa Bergnehr on teachers' responses to parental engagement all highlight the gap between expectations that teachers have of parents and the ability of parents to fulfil them. But, for the most part, these are also accompanied by a recognition of how the unequal allocation of material resources impacts on parents' ability to perform parenting. So, while cultivation of the right parenting practices is increasingly considered a necessity (Raemakers and Vandezande 2013) among professionals quoted in the chapters in this collection, it is also the case that the same practices are evaluated differently depending on who is doing them. There are numerous examples of how the same or a very similar practice may be recognised as good parenting in one context but not by another. So, sending your children to live away from home might not generally be recognised as a display of good parenting but might be considered good if, in the case of boarding schools, it was viewed as a common and unpro-blematic practice among certain elite groups. As Val Gillies (2010) has argued, it is those who are most powerful in society who determine domi-nant discourses over parenthood and therefore define which activities gain widespread traction. This variation between parents adds to our under-standing of the way in which material and cultural differences alongside changes in relationship and household situations impact on our doing of parenthood.

The reason why many of the current examples of good parenthood in the UK are education related is because the outcomes about which gov-ernment is most concerned, relate to achieving educational qualifications, which it is hoped can then be translated into labour market success. In other words, they are focused on children's development into future adults, well-becoming rather than well-being. Good parenthood is increasingly foregrounded in political discussions of how to promote social renewal and to ensure that poor children do not become poor adults. As childhood researchers have for some time argued, children's well-being needs to capture current quality of life rather than focusing solely on developmental aims, and capture subjective information from children themselves, as illustrated by UNICEF report cards (2013). This opens up the question of what doing good parenthood is intended to achieve. The change in terminology in this edited collection, from parenting to parenthood, reflects that it is important not to overstate the extent to which we are able to construct sets of activities that operate outside of institutional regimes (Gilding 2010). There are limits to parents' ability to invent ideas of good parenthood, and these chapters highlight how individual family members and others, such as social workers and teachers who have a level of authority over the actions of parents, construct appropriate parent-child interactions and respond to implicit normative understandings of how good parenthood should be performed.

IMPLICATIONS FOR FUTURE THINKING

Centrality of Parent-Child Relationships

Academic social scientists need to engage with the normative in order to reflect that we constantly find examples of individuals and families negotiating good and bad parenthood in empirical studies: to sidestep this is a failure of take seriously the accounts of participants in the real world. What brings together the chapters in this collection is the commitment to the parent-child relationship, and it is the exposition of how this works in the everyday that underpins accounts of good parenthood practice and cultural ideals. Reflexivity needs to be situated in the knowledge and understanding of an established and ongoing relationship, and specific parental practices are effective only when seen within the context of a broad caring and emotional commitment.

An intimate, engaged relationship includes both care in the present and concern for the future. Therefore, centring the parent-child relationship allows for changes in the practices and displays of parenthood to occur over time as relationships are dynamic. Focusing on a relationship also acknowledges that parents are not simply conduits for care, as care and love are not unidirectional but flow between parents and children. In Dannesboe's chapter on how children talk about good parents, it is striking that what is valued is a combination of knowledge, solidarity, and engagement (albeit at the right level of intensity). The chapter by Sparrman et al analyses familial togetherness in children's museums and amusement parks and documents how parenthood involves actors and networks that are usually overlooked by family research. Westerling's discussion of "parenting together apart" illustrates how divorce does not dissolve the family relations that is constituted by parenthood. Doing good parenthood, as developed in this volume, represents a meeting of child studies and family studies, which takes seriously the view that parents and children construct each other. Parent-child relationships then produce the "familial relationship goods" that people need to flourish (Brighouse and Swift 2014).

Working with Displaying Families

The discussion of doing good parenthood also provides a contribution to developing the concept of *displaying family*. In developing Morgan's (1996, 2011) *family practices*, Finch's concept took account of the way in which others responded to family activities and interacted with the central protagonist's behaviour. In response to her invitation to use and debate displaying families, the idea was opened out, and contested. First, it was highlighted by a number of the authors (Haynes and Dermott 2011; McIntosh et al. 2011; Seymour 2011) that displays of families require reciprocity in order for them to be successful. That is, displays do not occur in a vacuum and so if other family members fail to acknowledge their existence, authenticity or appropriateness then they have not accomplished the work of showing that "this is my family and it works" (Finch 2007). Second, and relatedly, that the displays are not just produced and dedicated towards other family members but can be directed voluntarily towards outside agencies and also even be required by powerful external parties (for example, immigration authorities, Carver 2014).

More focused attention on parenthood provides insights for thinking through all three pertinent issues. Parenthood is a fruitful domain for the idea of contested displays precisely because there is such debate over how "it" should be done. While principles of ensuring that children are physically safe, emotionally secure, and usefully prepared for the future all resonant across the accounts, there is acute disagreement over how the relative importance of well-being versus well-becoming (present versus future orientation) should be negotiated in practice, which is accessible in people's accounts of their thinking. There is also a sense of how parents may have to negotiate differences of opinion over ideals and practices. The chapters show how contestation, diverging views, or simply just different practices in enacting good parenthood are played out in everyday life. The role of external others, who lie outside of the immediate set of family members with whom the original article by Finch (2007) was most concerned, is also very much alive in these chapters. While the issue of an internal process of reflexive thinking is highlighted, there is also a strong sense of how displays of good parenthood are not governed solely by parental responses and interpretations of broad cultural prescriptions but of the powerful role exerted by external agencies. The process of dialogue between parents, and parents and others is inflected with a need to respond in some way to the authority of those who have particular responsibility and control over specific aspects of children's lives.

As these chapters illustrate, the idea of doing good parenthood is not one that is simply being imposed on individual parents as an abstract concept but instead is worked with and interpreted. As a whole, this collection of work is inspiring not only for its intellectual rigour and detailed empirical analysis but also in prompting broader thinking about the value of pursuing ideas of doing good parenthood.

REFERENCES

Brighouse, H., and A. Swift. 2014. *Family values: The ethics of parent-child relationships.* Princeton: Princeton University Press.

Carver, N. 2014. "Displaying genuineness: Cultural translation in the drafting of marriage narratives for immigration applications and appeals." *Families, Relationships and Societies* 3: 271–286.

Dermott, E., and M. Pomati. 2016. "'Good' parenting practices: How important are poverty, education and time pressure?" *Sociology* 50(1): 125–142.

Faircloth, C., and E. Lee. 2010. "Introduction: Changing parenting culture" *Sociological Research Online* 15(4). http://www.socresonline.org.uk/15/4/1.html. Accessed 16 May 2016.

Field, F. 2010. *The foundation years: Preventing poor children becoming poor adults.* London: Cabinet Office.

Finch, J. 2007. "Displaying families." *Sociology* 41: 65–81.

Giddens, A. 1998. *The transformation of intimacy.* Cambridge: Polity Press.

Gilding, M. 2010. "Reflexivity over and above convention: The new orthodoxy in the sociology of personal life, formerly sociology of the family." *British Journal of Sociology* 61(4): 757–777.

Gillies, V. 2010. "Is poor parenting a class issue? Contextualising anti-social behaviour and family life." In *Is parenting a class issue?* edited by M. Klett-Davies, 44–61. London: Family and Parenting Institute.

Haynes, J., and E. Dermott. 2011. "Displaying mixedness." In *Displaying families,* edited by E. Dermott and J. Seymour, 145–159. Basingstoke: Palgrave Macmillan.

McIntosh, I., N. Dorrer, S. Punch, and R. Emond. 2011. "I know we can't be a family, but as close as you can get: Displaying families within an institutional context." In *Displaying families*, edited by E. Dermott and J. Seymour, 175–196. Basingstoke: Palgrave Macmillan.

Morgan, D. 1996. *Family connections: An introduction to family studies*. Cambridge: Polity.

Morgan, D. 2011. *Rethinking family practices*. Basingstoke: Palgrave Macmillan.

Raemakers, S., and A. Vandezande. 2013. "'Parents need to become independent problem solvers': A critical reading of the current parenting culture through the case of Triple P." *Ethics and Education* 8(1): 77–88.

Seymour, J. 2011. "Family hold back: Displaying families in the single-location home/workplace." In *Displaying families*, edited by E. Dermott and J. Seymour, 160–174. London: Palgrave Macmillan.

UNICEF. 2013. *Child Well-being in Rich Countries: A Comparative Overview*. Florence: UNICEF.

Esther Dermott, Ph.D. is Professor of Sociology at the University of Bristol, UK. A sociologist of family life, her research examines the culture, practices and policies associated with contemporary parenthood, and interrogates dominant views and measures of "good parenting". Her most recent work includes analysis of the relationship between parenting and poverty and a special issue of *Families, Relationships and Societies* on patterns of change and continuity in fatherhood.

INDEX

© The Author(s) 2016   149
A. Sparrman et al. (eds.), *Doing Good Parenthood*, Palgrave Macmillan
Studies in Family and Intimate Life, DOI 10.1007/978-3-319-46774-0